UNDERTAKII
UNDERT

TRUE STORIES OF BEING LAID TO REST

BY

STANLEY SWAN

www.bookstandpublishing.com

Published by
Bookstand Publishing
Morgan Hill, CA 95037
4233_2

ISBN 978-1-63498-049-4

Printed in the United States of America

ACKNOWLEDGEMENTS

I want to offer huge gratitude to a number of persons who have given me encouragement, support and advice in the long process of making this book a reality. First to my wife Sandra who for thirty years has helped me in making crucial decisions and supporting me in my efforts.

To my family, my brothers Ed and Gary and sister Mary Jane for being great siblings....they are the best!

To Mom and Dad, the late Robert and Frances Swan, better parents no one has ever had.

To my friend and supporter Bryan Hills of Hills Monument Studio, Park Ave. in Corning, N.Y.

hillsmonumentstudio@stny.rr.com

And to the most wonderful manuscript editor of all; Jenica Drehmer. without Jenica's skills this book would not have happened, I shall always be indebted to her.

Jenica Drehmer is a wife, a mother, a writer, an editor, a college professor, an academic advisor, and a learning coach. She has followed her love of language and literature around the world. Jenica has her BA in English and her MA in English, both from SUNY New Paltz. She resides in Corning, NY with her husband and two daughters. Jenica can be reached at: jenicabd@gmail.com.

FOREWORD

*I*t's probably pretty obvious from a glance at the title to surmise what this book is all about. For many generations 'undertakers' have been tending to the needs of the general public in their time of loss and grief. The funeral profession is one that is often shunned, not talked about, avoided, and many times made fun of. But of all the professions, it is probably one of the most rewarding. This book and the stories therein are a compilation of almost 36 years spent in the industry. The stories are all true, no fiction, as they used to say on TVs' Dragnet "just the facts ma'am", and that is indeed what we will be engaged in here.

This book will share some gut wrenching stories of untimely death and the agony felt by survivors...accidental death, homicide, suicide, death as a result of mother nature...and on the flip side... incredibly humorous stories of people doing what they do best... just being themselves while in awkward situations.

From a quiet death in a rural farm house... to the recovery of humans caught in 911 and the wrath of Hurricane Katrina...this book relates it all. The writer; Stanley E Swan and his wife Sandra spent 20 years operating a small rural funeral home in rural New York State. The stories here represent his work there, and at several other funeral homes around New York. The names in the stories have been changed to protect the bereaved and their privacy.

We publish this book with the utmost humility, respect and regard for the families we have served. We hope it will give you an insight into what people in funeral service do on a daily basis to serve their communities.

Your assignment: settle into your favorite chair, shut off the phone, And let's begin to wander thru the Undertakings of an Undertaker; True stories of being laid to rest.

CONTENTS

CHAPTER ONE
BORN TO BE AN UNDERTAKER

It wasn't hard to grow up in the 50's and 60's in rural Jasper, New York. There were rich farm lands, where you could ride your bike and not worry about strangers, where you could leave your doors unlocked and know things would be in place when you returned, where you could feed an occasional hobo walking down Route 17, knowing that he would not do you or your family harm. It was a place of real simplicity, innocence, and hard work.

Being one kid of four on a dairy farm in this small town was fantastic! Finding the cows for the evening milking, bailing hay and stowing it in the barn, fixing fences and getting in grandpa's firewood were chores that seemed endless, both in time and fun. There was plenty of work to go around for myself, brothers Ed and Gary and sister Mary Jane.

You felt alive. You felt good. You felt rewarded. The fields were green and lush. The cats scrambled from the rafters in the barn when you rattled their milk dish. The kids jockeyed the apples down the creek with sticks in a weekly "apple drive." Could anything be better than this?

Adjacent to our property was and still stands the Jasper Five Corners Cemetery. What a wondrous place to visit and play as a child. We hid amongst the tall leaning grave markers, running and scooting amongst the stones while the graves inhabitants gave no heed to the noise overhead made by us. It was on one such outing that my brother Gary had the unfortunate incident of one of those large grave markers give way. As he lay on the ground in agony, we saw that his leg had been laid wide open. And, as kids do, we ran to

1

the house as fast as we could, yelling for mom to come to the rescue. After a trip to the doctor and many stitches later, we received the proper lectures about not playing in the cemetery. Maybe this could mean more chores if it seemed we didn't have enough to keep us occupied? Maybe we should regroup and re-consider our strategy for future outings? These were our mother's questions, not ours. The cemetery was only fifty yards from the house. We didn't have to take the bus to get there. It was a quick bike ride or walk to the entrance, and we all knew would be back another day.

The author at the Five Corners Cemetery in Jasper, New York, doing some family genealogy gathering.

It was on another beautiful Autumn day in October when I noticed the shiny big black hearse turn past our house and head for "our" cemetery. We considered it "ours" because we had three generations of our family buried there, and it was a frequent event to go to those graves, read the stones and wonder about those who had gone before us and what they must have they been like. Why did they die so young? Were their caskets buried deep? Did we look like them? So many questions, but they would have to wait. There would be another time for those matters. The most pressing question was, "What is this hearse doing here?"

I crept behind a small stone and watched with searching eyes as the hearse made its way up the dirt driveway past tall maple trees ready to drop their magnificent orange leaves. The hearse stopped at the corner, the driver emerged, and I smiled because I knew him. It was okay; he was the local undertaker from six miles down the road. I relaxed, straightened, and walked to where a mound of dirt overlooked an open grave. As I looked down into the awaiting concrete box in the ground, I thought, what a shame to be buried on such a fine day: bright blue sky, puffy clouds, a light breeze blowing the fallen leaves into the nearby fence...

The undertaker and I exchanged peasantries as he and the digger lowered the casket into the ground with rough gray ropes that were snugged around the handles. Before the casket hit the bottom of the box, I noticed a newspaper on the floor of the vault. It must have been a leftover from when the vault was made and readied for burial. Someday that will be very interesting reading for someone if this man should ever by dug up. It was like this man had his own time capsule beneath him. The grave was quickly covered, and as I watched the grave digger throw the last shovel of dirt on the grave and light his pipe, I thought, "I could do this someday. I could be the one tucking the dead to rest." For a long time, I thought about that man, awakening someday, finding that newspaper, reliving the headlines and the weather of that October day in 1965.

The hearse drove out of the driveway. The digger had his tools in his truck. The temporary marker had been set on the grave, and its occupant had started his eternal slumber with those around him who had gone before. I headed for the house. The light was fading, and it would soon be supper time. It was a good day for a burial, but how did I know that? I was only a kid.

3

Examples of early embalming fluids used in the 1940s and 1950s.

CHAPTER TWO
THE SPARROW

A re we born to do certain things, to perform certain tasks? Are we destined before birth to be what is planned for us in advance? Many scholars and theologians believe so. As an adolescent riding a bike down a country road, you would think that death and dying would be the furthest thing from my young mind. It was my daily routine as a kid to sit on my bike under a large maple tree at the end of our sidewalk and watch the cars going by on the "main" road and then ride as fast as possible down the dirt road to the bridge two hundred yards away. At the tender age of eight, I found a dead sparrow near the road, and I came to a grinding halt, throwing cinders up as the brakes locked the back wheel.

What a sad day to find a beautiful sparrow, rich in brown, gray and black, lying lifeless and begging for attention from a passerby like myself. Gently taking the sparrow to a nearby lilac tree near the road and placing him tenderly in the green pasture, I knew I had to give this sparrow a proper departure. So, back at the house, I constructed a small cardboard box complete with a scrap of cloth that I had found. Soon, I placed the sparrow in the box, and upon the lid I placed a small aromatic bloom of that wonderful lilac. It felt good to take care of that poor bird. He did not deserve this death, but he did deserve this final resting place.

I'm sure I wasn't the only youngster who had ever buried a dead animal or bird, but was it foretelling of things to come? I couldn't contemplate that now. I had a Little League game to get to, and as the second baseman, I had to be there on time. It was a fifteen minute bike ride to the school and the coach would be rallying the team for tonight's game.

I would visit that sparrow's grave in the days ahead and place a cross on it made of two sticks and a piece of string. The task had been completed. It was one more of my life's ingredients into building a career that in two decades would be knocking on my door for full time attention for decades to come.

The author on the way into school at Simmons in Syracuse, New York, in the spring of 1980.

CHAPTER THREE
BURIAL IN NOWHERE

Most people have an idea of where they are going to end up, that is, whether they are going to be buried, cremated, donated to science, whatever. And most of those who have chosen burial for themselves or a significant other usually have a final place in mind, a "new address", as my father used to say. That "new address" could be in a very elite metropolitan, multi-acre cemetery where no expense is spared for an appropriate spot to spend eternity. In some cases, you can even reside next to someone who is famous, or infamous. Up to a few short years ago, you could even buy a crypt next to Marilyn Monroe. But for most folks of average or meager incomes, a simple burial plot will suffice. Many choose to buy several lots at once, all in a row, guaranteeing family members will be buried together, no matter where life may physically take them across the country or across the world.

In our small town of roughly one thousand, most burials were made in three main cemeteries. There was the Catholic cemetery, operated by the local Catholic church, and two other non-denominational cemeteries, all within two miles of each other. Then there were over two dozen little private cemeteries scattered amongst the hillsides and tucked between old broken down barns and houses, some containing only a few graves dating back one to two hundred years.

So the choices were pretty fair for people in this rural town. You could try to locate yourself "in town" in one of the main cemeteries, or consider going out into the wilderness for a more remote and serene setting. Most all cemeteries have a sexton, a person who is in charge of the cemetery. He or she keeps the maps, the deeds, the records of burials made, etc.. The sexton's job is not an easy one, especially in regards to old cemeteries where records are sketchy, or in some cases, non-existent.

It was a lazy day one summer when we received a death call from a lady in a nearby town, just a few miles to the east. Her husband, in his mid-fifties, had died suddenly, and she was not quite sure how to proceed with his disposition. At the time of the arrangements, she enlightened us to the fact that her husband had said he wanted to be buried in the Woodbury cemetery, upon the hill, just three miles from our funeral home. I had never heard of this cemetery, so I started making inquiries of local officials about it to ascertain who might be in charge, what it cost to open a grave there, etc.. Few townspeople had ever heard of it and suggested I contact another funeral director some fifteen miles away whom they were sure had made a burial there before. I heeded their advice and phoned my competitor and asked him about the Woodbury Cemetery. What he told me shocked me.

"There's really no one in charge of that cemetery, so if that guy wants to be buried there, go up, find a spot, dig a grave and then take the burial permit down to the town clerk in Greenwood."

"Um," I thought. This is starting to sound a bit like Boot Hill in the old West: no one in charge, just go bury the guy, call it a day. He assured me this was the real deal, so after putting the phone down, I decided that tomorrow I would take my map and a cemetery hunting we would go.

The next morning, I awoke early, thinking most of the night about what I would discover at Woodbury, if indeed I could locate it at all. I piled into the funeral home station wagon, coffee in hand, and headed East on old route 17. The location, according to my funeral friend, was just a few short miles from where I was and up an old country road. Taking his directions in hand, I made the appropriate turns to where I thought it would be...and nothing. I

8

back tracked twice, no, maybe three times, and in desperation decided to continue my hunt on foot, so I pulled the wagon to the side and piled out. I walked down the dirt road, actually having to watch my footing on the semi-steep decline, when I spotted the culvert driveway leading into the woods. There were no "Do Not Trespass" signs or mail boxes. Could this be it?

I walked into the marshy road that was still quite wet, even though summer had been on us over a month now. About fifty yards in and after a sharp right hand turn, there it was. The cemetery looked about a hundred yards square, quite small by comparison to the "townies" I was used to burying in. There were a few small trees growing and lumps of dark grass and brush, but no visible headstones. As I made my way closer and kicked away the shrubs, small stones started to appear. This cemetery was being taken over very quickly by Mother Nature, and there was no evidence of any recent burial, for what appeared to be decades. As I navigated from grave to grave, I started to look for the family name of the man who I was to bury in just two short days. I made quick notes on a pad I had in my pocket, but found nothing near the name that would soon be added to this lonely and desolate place.

After a twenty to thirty minute search, there was still no family name even close to the family I was currently serving. So now what? Do I just play a game of eenie-meenie-minie-moe and pick a spot? Not a real personal touch in picking out the final resting place for this gentleman. It was time to retreat, go back to the funeral home, and regroup. I only wanted to bury this fellow once, so the spot had to be right, not for me, but for his family. Twenty minutes later, I was on the phone questioning the family further about his grave lot. They told me pretty much the same as the other funeral director had told me. Just pick out a spot; no particular reference points were necessary. I now had permission from all concerned, so why did I still have this lingering question in my mind?

The next day, I contacted one of my local construction guys who would help me from time to time opening graves. As he backed his tractor off the back of his trailer and headed up the rough road to the cemetery, I thought about the loneliness and isolation of this spot. It was dreadful and dreary, adjectives that really didn't describe fully this clearing in the woods that had been established years ago to hold human beings. My hired construction guy, Bill, started to dig ever so slowly with his backhoe, not knowing what may lie beneath the thick layers of dead grass, leaves and twigs. The soil was almost black as the entered the earth itself, very rich looking soil indeed, for good reason. Decades of forest tree droppings and plant and animal contributions had made for a wonderful soil to dig in, despite the occasional small tree root. The grave digger continued to plunge the backhoe bucket into the ground, digging the grave deeper, piling the fresh virgin soil next to the hole that would, within a day or so, be home for my newly deceased customer. After about forty minutes, our work was done. Bill advised me that he probably would trailer his tractor and come back after the funeral to fill the grave. He didn't feel comfortable leaving the machine way out in nowhere with no supervision. I agreed and completely understood his concern. It was interesting to think that I was willing to leave my customer here, but Bill was worried about leaving his machine.

With the grave now selected and opened, we were pretty much ready to proceed with our funeral. The following day, the family made it into the funeral home on time, the minister was very brief in his remarks, and within thirty short minutes the service had concluded, and we were ready to make the short drive to Woodbury for the final internment. The wife of the deceased had decided that only she, a couple of the sons, and a couple of nephews would be going to the cemetery. She wanted it to be quiet, serene, private and not "showy" in any way. Simple is good. It takes less preparation and is a whole lot less stressful on everyone concerned. Thirty minutes later, we were there, up the dirt road, into the small secluded cemetery, being very careful in passing by the few small stones, many still buried in forest foliage. In keeping with an old tradition, the family wanted to stay as we physically lowered the casket into the ground and into the concrete grave liner which was already in place. In a few moments, this was completed. The family had disembarked, and I sat quietly on an old stump nearby, waiting for the grave digger to re-appear with his tractor to backfill the grave. After the grave had been filled, I placed the temporary grave marker into the fresh soil, signifying who was now there, with name, date of birth and death. I wondered how long it would be before the forest grasses and weeds would take over this new site and obscure it from future visitors. It probably wouldn't take long.

As I pulled out of the cemetery, my eyes caught the sight of two black crows coming into nest. They were to be the sentries that would now watch over this quiet place, this burial ground with no human tasked to watch over it. I'm sure they wondered who I was and what my business was within the confines of their space. Their offspring would probably be witness to a future burial here, and they would probably wonder the same. The scene was full green and brown with only the brilliant red of the flower piece which now sat atop the new grave. I'm sure the sentries would look at that for days ahead, contemplating the new look of their forest floor.

CHAPTER FOUR

REMAINS OF THE GENESEE RIVER KILLER

From 1988 to 1990, the city of Rochester, in Monroe County, N.Y., suffered at the hands of a serial killer. Those in that beautiful part of New York would never have imagined such a rash of brutal crimes taking place there. The victims, mostly prostitutes and women of the street, were snatched, taken to secluded areas, beaten and/or strangled, and their bodies dumped within thirty miles of the downtown city limits. For months, authorities hunted for the killer and finally received a break when the killer was actually spotted near the scene of one of his last killings. He was apprehended, convicted and sentenced. His name was Arthur Shawcross. Shawcross died in prison, but his deadly killing spree in upstate New York is remembered and re-hashed regularly by law enforcement and members of the justice system. It was an eerie day when this writer came in contact with one of his victims, a day that still gives me chills when it is reviewed in my mind. The following is from the notes I made the day I met one of his victims.

I hadn't planned on going to the medical examiner's office that day. Our local coroner had pronounced a fellow dead at home who had not been seeing a doctor regularly, so it was pretty much cut and dry that the body would have to go to the medical examiner in Rochester for an autopsy. Our local county did not have a forensic pathologist, so all cases referred by the coroner had to be transported by vehicle, eighty-five miles to the north. It was cold, and a winter wind was blowing pretty good, but the roads were passable for sure, even with the brief gusts that would billow some light snow on my path from time to time as I steered my black Suburban northward over the hard gray asphalt.

In the two hour trip to Rochester, I always had a lot to think about. Would the pathologist on duty take just blood and fluids? Would he require a full autopsy, which could take several hours? Would he send me home to come back tomorrow? About an hour into the trip, I encountered my first delay of the day; an 18-wheeler had jackknifed and blocked part of the north bound lanes. Wonderful. The sheriff's deputy in the middle of the road putting down a flare as I eased closer had that "I'd rather be home watching football today look" as I rolled down my window to inquire about the stop.

"Shouldn't be too long," he blurted.

I rolled up my Suburban window as a good blast of wintry air came at me from the west. I turned on the radio to check the conditions from here into the city and heard nothing threatening, so I eased back into my seat and reached for my coffee thermos, which I always took on the road. And if I remembered correctly, there should be a Dunkin stop coming up in twenty-five miles or so. Ah, my spot indeed. I must know where every Dunkin Donuts is east of the Mississippi. I should have purchased stock years ago. Why do I procrastinate when I know something is so good? Back to reality…

The deputy was right; the delay didn't last long. Within five minutes or so, my vehicle, my deceased on the stretcher in the back, and I had resumed our motoring northward. Mmm, just past noon. I should arrive at the medical examiner's by 1-1:30, hopefully a quick turn around, and I could actually be home by dark, which in this part of the world in winter is usually between 4:30 and 5:00 pm. As I rounded the back of the medical examiner's office, it appeared to be quite busy for a Sunday afternoon; usually the place is deserted. What appeared to be two unmarked police cars shadowed each other as the crisp wind swirled around the entrance doors. I punched the outdoor buzzer expecting a quick "Can I help you?" A minute or two went by, when finally a sullen voice said, "Yep. Be right there." The speaker went lifeless.

So here I was, on a nice wintry day, standing at the medical examiner's with my deceased all tucked in on my stretcher, awaiting an entrance into the world of forensic science. Within a couple of minutes, the attendant had hit the bar on the fire door, and I was wheeling in my charge, past one of the coroner's removal wagons, which was covered in some mud and road debris, looking like it had just been out on a run.

"Busy day?" I inquired as the attendant sat at his computer screen and started punching his keyboard.

"Oh yeah," he replied and continued, "big time stuff going on today...real big stuff."

I wondered what that referred to. Had there been a multi-fatality traffic accident? Major fire in the city? Multiple homicides all brought in at once? We completed the paperwork quickly to log in my remains, and I had started to prepare to move my deceased to the attendant's table for prints and photography when my eye glanced into the next room. Surrounding a stainless steel exam table were two guys in white shirts and ties, all wearing latex exam gloves, one with a camera, one with a clipboard. They chatted to each other, then refocused on the table itself.

"Want to take a look?" asked the attendant. He didn't have to ask me twice. In a quick ten steps, I was at the foot of the exam table stretching my neck to its breaking point, my eyes going wide and focusing.

My first impression was that these guys weren't pathologists. They didn't have the bio garb on, and they just didn't look the part. No, these guys were cops, better yet, detectives. The serious looks on their faces were like stone on Mt. Rushmore. One actually looked like Joe Friday on *Dragnet*. That was scary in itself. Now, what do I do here, introduce myself? Be still and play stupid? Start asking questions? I opted for the first. They weren't impressed that I was a funeral director and member of a local sheriff's department eighty-five miles to the south, although the latter statement did have some weight with the older of the trio.

"Alright," he muttered, "Just don't get close or touch anything alright?"

All of our eyes returned to the stainless steel table, brilliantly lit by an overhead spotlight. My eyes raced from top to bottom, then right to left, trying to determine what I was looking at. Bones. I see bones. I see some other artifacts, some tufts of hair. Whoever this was, they had been deceased for some time, and it was impossible to tell from first glance if they were male or female.

"This is one of them we think," blurted the guy closest to me.

"One of them," I thought to myself. One of them? Let's see now. Rochester N.Y…skeletal remains…Rochester N.Y.. Every muscle in me instantly froze. I caught my breath. My gut did a flip.

"This is one of the victims of the Genesee River killer," I said in a very low and subdued voice.

"We think so," came the response, "We think the remains are female. She was found last night."

The two detectives made some quick notes on small spiral notebooks they had taken out, then quickly tucked them back into their sports coats.

"Put her away for tonight. The Dr. said he'd start his work in the morning. Maybe we can make out something from this one. Not much for him to work with, but maybe we'll get lucky."

The two made their way out of the medical examiner's office, as I stood motionless at the exam table, looking closer now to see what I could recognize as familiar. There was a vertebral column for sure, roughly thirty inches long, pale and grey in color and weathered from what looked like months of outdoor exposure. Several small bones, looking to be from either a foot or hand, lay near the spinal column, several small patches or clumps of dark brown or black hair

16

entwined one of the small bones. Ah, here was something familiar: a cassette recording tape. This would be of great interest to police. It, too, was covered in mud and grass and showing long exposure to the elements. And finally, there was what appeared to be two small pieces of jewelry chain, perhaps from a wrist or necklace.

I wondered if this person would ever be identified. Were they male or female? Would they be able to determine a cause of death? It seemed unlikely. There wasn't much here to work with. I also wondered what went through this person's thoughts, minutes, or perhaps just moments, before death. And was it at the hands of the Genesee River killer? If this was one of his victims, she would be like the others, between the ages of twenty and forty, living on the streets with not much future. But no one, living on the street or not, deserved to end up here, on a stainless steel table with a Jane Doe tag and an ID number to match the date and time found.

The answers to my questions probably would come in time, but for tonight, my day was at an end. I nodded to the attendant, grabbed my paperwork, and headed for the exit door. As I headed my car south with the empty stretcher on board, my mind kept reviewing what I had just witnessed. The remains of some unknown human were now held in cold storage at the medical examiner's office. Who was that person? How had they died? What were their last thoughts before things went dark forever? The chill that came over me was amplified as I turned the wiper blades on high. The snow was coming fast now. My trip home might be a challenging one. The chill that was the Genesee River killer stayed with me, all the way home.

CHAPTER FIVE

STARS AND STRIPES, ALMOST LOST

The funeral had gone very well for the elderly gentleman. A veteran of World War II and a member of many local veterans' groups, he had garnered a large number of people to visit him at the funeral home, and his widow and family were very pleased with the turnout.

As the minister gave the final prayer and retreated from the podium, I advanced and gave the final instructions, telling all that we would be heading to the cemetery for a brief committal service and for military honors to be accorded there. As the chapel emptied out, my assistant and I sorted the flowers that would be making the short two mile trip with the casket to the cemetery. I quickly reviewed my check list: what was to stay in the casket, what was to come out, and which flowers were to go. I put my paperwork in my coat pocket; all was in order. The rose tan crepe interior was folded around the deceased, and I gently closed the top of the oak casket over the gentleman, my eyes doing a quick final scan to make sure all was well with him. The lid latch was secured, and we were ready to disembark.

The drive with the funeral procession was a short one, just a couple of miles or so to the little cemetery where many of his family had been buried before him. It was cold, and a light rain was falling, but that wouldn't be a deterrent. We had a tent over the open grave, and the green all weather carpet and folding chairs were in place and awaiting their occupants.

As we opened the back of the hearse, the military honor guard, two gentlemen in their dress blues, came to attention and full salute as our bearers moved the casket under the tent and onto the lowering device. The device was a great invention of the 20th century, designed to hold the casket on two heavy duty straps, and, at the appropriate time, with a flick of a switch, it would lower the casket ever so slowly to its final resting place some six feet below.

The casket was in place, the flag full opened and draped over it. The family sat quietly as we directed the others to get close under the tent to escape the light rain and to hear the final commendation of the minister. Standing next to the family, I looked across the casket to the far side and the military at full attention awaiting their turn to remove, fold, and present the flag to the mourning, but thankful family.

When the minister had finished, he stepped aside, the waiting soldiers in dark blue and pressed white shirts stepped to the casket, one at the head, one at the foot, and removed the flag. Stepping carefully three feet to the south, they proceeded to fold the flag in a very dignified and reverent manner.

As the gentleman stood with a firm grip on the blue field, his counterpart started the small folds of the red and white, as he worked his way toward the field. Then the inconceivable happened. The soldier with the red and white in hand simply disappeared. It was though the earth had swallowed him up. I glanced quickly to the soldier at the head of the casket. His gaze was directly down and his face stern and concerned at the same time.

I stepped to my left around the foot end of the casket, and for the first time in thirty years, I observed a military officer still standing, but three foot below ground level. He was still holding the red and white field, but the flag was now at a sixty degree angle to the soldier at the head of the casket. I bent down and asked the soldier if he was alright. He did not reply. Such true dedication and professionalism I had never seen. The sunken soldier continued to fold the flag as his feet tried to grab the side of the grave which had a firm grip on him. He soon emerged. His right side was wet and dirty.

The flag had never become dislodged, had never touched the earth. I was sure he had been injured, but we would address that later, not now.

The flag folding continued, and the presentation was made to the widow. The taps were played, and all emerged from the cemetery like nothing unusual had happened that day. The soldier called later that day and apologized to me and the family, but I told him the family had called first, and that they were concerned for his possible injuries, and they thanked him for his service. Only a few scrapes and bruises were sustained, which was a lucky break indeed for the young man. I noted in my journal that week, what a wonderful display of professionalism by these two men of the military, and I thought how lucky our country was to have them on our side and by our side.

CHAPTER SIX

SHE SAID WHAT?

People never cease to amaze those of us in funeral service. Just when you think there can't be any new scenario, someone will step up and smack you upside the head with a "you've got to be kidding me" idea, suggestion, or question. And, so, on this sunny afternoon, I drove our funeral lead car with five family cars following closely into the entrance of the cemetery. A co-worker and I had arrived earlier, set up our small service tent over the grave, put down some green carpet grass and a half dozen chairs. It was to be an urn burial today, so the grave was quite small, only fifteen inches side to side and front to back, and twenty inches deep. The fellow who opened the graves for us had this one finished in time, as usual, and had covered it with a piece of plywood.

The family had not arranged for a minister today, and had asked me in advance if I could offer a few prayers at graveside for their mother. I told them that I would be honored. I walked to the graveside, placed the beautiful gold and black spun bronze urn on the urn table over the grave, and started to seat the family for what I was assured would be a brief service. After reading some scripture and doing a few closing prayers, I asked members of the family if they wished to speak about the dearly departed, and many stood up, taking about fifteen minutes. It was a beautiful day, and no one was really in a hurry, so the pace seemed to take a natural course.

At the conclusion of the proceedings, the daughter who had made all of the arrangements, walked to the urn, reaching down and stroking it gently as a daughter might stroke her mother's face.

"It's such a lovely urn. The black and gold contrast is startling. I think Mom would have loved my choice."

I agreed. She had picked out a striking piece, and now it was just minutes from being entered into the rich dark brown soil which would hold it in place until the Second Coming.

"You know?" the daughter uttered suddenly.

"This may sound kind of crazy, but I don't think I want to bury Mom today. I think I want to take her home with me and keep her with me, for, well, I don't know for how long. Maybe until it's my turn to come here."

The fellow who opened the grave was standing about eight feet away, steadying one of the tent poles, as the wind had just picked up significantly. His eyes opened wide, and he looked at me in disbelief. His thoughts jumped the gap between us, and I read his lips as he said, "She said what?"

That's what she said, alright. She wanted to take her mom home with her. I explained to the daughter that she would have to forfeit the money to open the grave, as it couldn't be returned. She had no problem with that. The sexton who had collected the payment and burial permit when we entered the cemetery said, "This is a bit unusual, but no problem. The grave will be here when she's ready."

So the family loaded into their vehicles, with mom in her beautiful black and gold urn, and headed to parts unknown. We started to retrieve our equipment and fold up the tent. As the grave digger directed his wheelbarrow over the grave and started back filling, he shook his head in disbelief.

"I never filled an empty one before."

It was another first, but it had been a simple and meaningful service. The family had made their tributes to their family member and had said their goodbyes, well, their almost goodbyes. Their final goodbyes will come when they are ready, but I know I won't be there for it, and I don't need to be. Their process and their way of finding peace is exactly that: theirs.

CHAPTER SEVEN

MOST UNUSUAL REQUESTS

Y ou never know what a family member is going to request of you when you are talking to them about burying a loved one and what they want to bury with them. The tradition of burying a loved one with artifacts, letters, favorite items, etc. actually started with the Egyptians... when their mummies were tucked away in secret chambers surrounded by a vast amount of gold, personal items, statues, and even stores of food for the afterlife. The custom remains today but the amount of actual items being buried has been reduced; however, the range of items buried today reflects the same categories of the ancients.

It was on a fine afternoon that a woman was making funeral arrangements for her husband. As most people know, when a person is put in a casket for viewing today, a majority of caskets are what we call "half couch," that is, once the deceased is dressed and put in the casket, only half of the casket is open for viewing. The bottom lid is closed and a piece of interior is draped over the deceased at about the mid line so viewers only see from the waist up.

As I sat in the arrangements room chatting with the widow, the subject of his clothes came up. She looked at me and said, "I only have a nice blue sport coat, white shirt and red tie. He doesn't need pants does he?"

Well, here was another first. "Well," I explained, "I guess you wouldn't need to put pants on him, seeing that the bottom of the casket is closed, and technically no one would know other than you and I that he didn't have any on."

The woman gave me a small grin and continued, "Well, I can't see putting pants on him. It's just more expense, and well, knowing him, he wouldn't be totally shocked going out with his knees showing."

I forced myself not to laugh out loud, the back of my throat straining to keep the sound within. "Well, let's just plan on that then," I said as I flipped through the last of the documents for her to sign.

The day of the funeral arrived. The friends and family of the deceased filed by the casket giving all due respects, and the minister made some comment about the deceased always being one who would "give his shirt off his back" to anyone in need. Little did he know that the shirt was not the article that was missing!

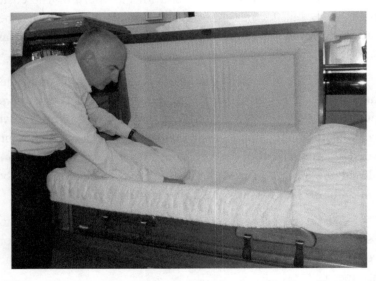

The author prepares a new casket in the merchandise room prior to meeting with a family.

CHAPTER EIGHT
THE TRAGEDY OF 9–11

Sept. 11, 2001. The funeral home was quiet that week, and on this day that would become one of the darkest in the nation's history, I was on duty with the county sheriff's office. Today would be one of those twice yearly deals where all officers would have to report to the firing range, to test their skills with weapons. In order to carry a weapon, you would have to qualify with your duty piece in handling, safety and accuracy of fire. How odd, I thought. Twice yearly, you had to show up, blow off maybe one hundred rounds and prove that, if you had to, you were capable of taking another's life in a desperate situation. No one in our department had ever had to do that, and I thought, "Here I am a mild mannered undertaker playing with a glock 19, capable of delivering 11 rounds of deadly force to some perpetrator. Kind of a conflict of interest." Maybe I would get to shoot somebody, then who knows? I might be the guy who gets called to bury him three or four days later. I shrugged it off in passing, although the thought had been in the heads of some of my co-workers. They were always making funeral jokes when I was around. It was natural. Most people have a natural curiosity about and often sense of the great beyond and death in general. And the questions never seemed to stop. Do people actually sit up after they die? Do hair and fingernails really grow after they're buried? But, these questions can be tackled later. Today's the object was to put as many rounds into the mannequin target at 50 yards as possible before the gorilla man blew his whistle.

We were on the line and almost ready to commence fire, when one of our sergeants came barreling in with a sheriff's car, throwing loose cinders just yards from where we stood. He leapt out and ran to our location, white as a ghost. I thought, "This can't be good. This guy is usually pretty cool and collected, so something monstrous must be afoot. I couldn't have been more right, but I wish I had been wrong.

"A plane just ran into one of the trade towers in New York!" our sergeant exclaimed. He then turned, giving no further details, and was gone as quickly as he had arrived. We all jumped to our vehicles, turned the ignitions and started scanning the channels for news and information. And there it was, the announcer was almost panicked in his nervous speech, giving details of how a passenger airliner had moments before slammed into the World Trade Center, producing a large fire ball of flying glass, concrete and smoke. At that moment, my gut told me this was going to be far from the average qualifying day at the range.

Within minutes, we were sickened to hear that a second plane had found its mark in the twin towers of New York. We finished our range quickly, knowing that the incidents that had just occurred were going to affect each and every one of us in some way. We returned to the department. The main office was in a mad rush. The Sheriff, his undersheriff, and a couple of lieutenants were huddled near a television near his office gathering as much information as was possible. Between rounds, the officers on the jail floor were trying to absorb as much as was possible about what was transpiring in that big city, six hours to our east. We all knew one fact. This was no accident; the country was definitely under attack, but we didn't know who was responsible or if there would be more to come.

The next several days were kind of a maze as we all went about our work, still monitoring as much as possible of the events unfolding in the big apple. Hundreds, if not thousands, of people were missing: people who worked in the tower, firefighters, police officers and volunteers who ran into the buildings to save others from the nightmare of that beautiful September morning. It wasn't until ten days past the event that our Sheriff received the call. Departments and agencies of law enforcement around the country

30

were being summoned to New York City to provide security, logistics and other support to the overwhelmed city in distress. The sheriff put the word out that our agency would be sending five officers, including him, to assist and that the team would be leaving within a few short days. Knowing that my abilities as a funeral director would be welcomed to some degree, I asked the undersheriff, a big strapping man with white hair and a handlebar mustache, if I could be included in the detail. He agreed, knowing that the city would be looking for people like me with skills in dealing with death. And there was a lot of death. The latest counts were staggering: only a few people rescued and thousands missing. The security and recovery operation would take weeks, months perhaps. Our deployment plans were underway.

For the next seventy two hours, our department scurried in making plans and gathering supplies for the trip southeast to New York City. The time scheduled for the five officers going had to be filled, and there was determination of what uniforms, equipment, etc. would be taken. The Sheriff decided we would wear our black BDUs, battle dress uniforms, with hat, shirt, cargo pants and standard work boots. He was told that most of the clothes needed, boots, gloves, etc., would be issued on site once we arrived. Our duty was not specified yet. Would we be sitting security posts? Handling traffic control? None of us were sure of what we were about to embark on, but we were all anxious to pile into our cars and head southeast.

The morning of our departure was non-eventful. We were all dressed in our BDUs, and the two vehicles we were taking were marked four wheel drive Sheriff car-vans stuffed to the brim with our supplies, personal bags and equipment. A female officer came out to the parking lot, gathered us in a group and snapped a couple of pictures. She said we were part of history now, and the event had to be recorded as such. We joked about that, but in the back of our minds, we knew she stood correct in her assumption.

After the shutter clicked a couple of times, we were on the road, heading east on Route 86, beginning the six hour plus trip to the adventure of a lifetime. We were all anxious, nervous, each in our own mind trying to put it all in perspective. As a funeral director, I was thinking more forensically about what we would find. The television network pictures were indeed horrific. So many people were trapped, missing and presumed dead. It would be a huge shock to the system, going from rural Western New York into the pit of the beast, and literally maybe into the pit that once was the World Trade Center.

We hadn't been on the road twenty minutes when one of our deputies saw a house trailer being towed by a truck just ahead of us. As we went into the passing lane to the left, the trailer started weaving from side to side, making the pass impossible, and, of course, our deputy being a solid professional, and not wanting to miss writing some paper, hit the lights and siren and pulled the guy over. I looked in my rear view mirror and saw the car the sheriff was in pull up behind us and stop position, his hands up in the air in that "what is this all about" gesture.

I pushed the front passenger door open, and my first stride made its way towards the sheriff's car, while our deputy headed in the opposite direction toward the truck driver, adjusting his black hat to its appropriate spot. His face told me the guy was going to get at least a good talking to, even if no paper was to be produced. The sheriff was a little bit put out. He wanted to make good time heading to the city and not play cop on the way.

"What to hell is he doing?" demanded the sheriff.

"We almost got swiped in a pass. Dan thought he should at least see what's up with the guy…" I replied.

"Well, tell him to make it snappy" was the response. "We need to be in Manhattan late day."

As I made my way back to the traffic stop, I could tell Dan was giving the guy a 'good talking' to about the weave as he walked around the trailer giving it a visual inspection for tires, stickers, etc.

After our brief respite from the drive, we were again heading east on 86, chuckling about the stop and how Danny had done his duty to keep the public safe, and us from getting sideswiped. The next few hours were passed in pretty much boredom as we motored to our destination. An hour or so out of the city, we stopped at a rest area to get gas and grab a quick bite to eat. As we piled out of our two vehicles and strode into the eating establishment, I'm sure we looked quite threatening, all dressed in black from head to toe and making loud and heavy sounds as our boots hit the pavement. We were on a mission. We just weren't sure what the mission was yet, but it wouldn't be long now. Our anticipation heightened as we ate our last fries and again adjusted the cars on their eastward trek.

Ninety minutes later, we were there. The New York skyline was illuminated in the distance, a wondrous sight, no matter the reason for the visit. As we drove into the city, we saw a huge police presence, everywhere: NYPD cars, Sheriffs cars, NYS police cars, military vehicles. It looked like a law enforcement convention was underway and everyone had been invited. We parked our vehicles at Battery Park, blocks from the trade center. A light rain fell as we exited the vehicles. As we checked our badges and identifications, a national guard carrying an M-16 approached. Our first test was moments away.

The guard member was young, maybe mid-twenties, his helmet chin strap pulled tightly around a slightly rounded face.

"State your business" he grunted, his weapon extended across his chest. To his rear, another guard member stepped in as backup.

"We have orders to report for duty" said our sheriff, speaking in a command voice that we all knew and respected.

The guard stepped up, asked for our Identifications and we all fumbled with our wallets, flashing our sheriffs' i.d. badges as we stepped up to the guard's glaring flashlight.

"The command post is 100 yards from the center, dead on. Walk straight to center. Do not deviate from your course."

Our sheriff nodded, and we took off in giant strides. Straight ahead and lit in brilliant white light was what was left of the World Trade Center. It appeared to be fifteen to eighteen stories of rubble, smoke billowing from what seemed like dozens of exit points. We walked on. We were maybe three city blocks from the rubble pile. My heart was in my throat. I was entering an unkept cemetery, which now held over two thousand people who hadn't been found, let alone buried. I glanced at the other officers. All eyes were fixed on the approaching pile, all faces stone cold and serious.

In the last block, we stopped. The sight in front of us could not have been created in Hollywood. This was mass destruction at its zenith. As I looked up at nearby buildings, it was though a giant knife had sliced off the faces of the structures. You could look into offices exposed. There were chairs, desks, computers, many pieces hanging by wires and dangling in mid-air. Pipes were ruptured and dripping water. Papers were everywhere, reams and reams of paper adrift and in the air and on the ground. Only occasionally did you see anything else identifiable: an office chair, part of a filing cabinet, a computer keyboard. How was a falling building able to concentrate such crushing blows to everything within? My first thought was, "How will this ever be cleaned up?" My first conclusion was that it would take years, not months, to clean up the area.

As our group stood in amazement at the scene of the rubble pile, firemen and rescue workers continued working, looking for survivors. There were none to be found. This was twelve days after the fact, and the chances of anyone being found alive at this point were next to impossible. Suddenly, a rescue worker started waving a flag about fifty yards directly above us. This was followed by a short siren blast, and the remainder of those working in the "pile" stopped in their tracks. We ased an on duty officer what was going on, and he replied, "They've found another victim." Within minutes, a dozen rescue workers had made their way to the location, a firemen's rescue basket/gurney had been hoisted in position, and a victim's remains were placed in the basket and covered with an American flag. There was a lump in my throat the size of an apple as dozens of workers passed the basket carrying the remains downward, hand to hand, worker to worker, all handling the remains with extreme caution and due respect. Here was another firefighter or police officer recovered from this smoldering maze of concrete and steel. The basket was placed in the back of a waiting ambulance, which pulled away silently, as fellow officers wiped away tears and comforted each other. How many more would there be? How long would it take? How exhausted these men looked as they went back to their dreadful duty.

Suddenly, our sheriff did an about face and ordered us to retreat. We were off to Staten Island, where we were to stay and be briefed in the morning on our next several days of duties and assignments. The scenes of what we had just witnessed raced through my mind, and I knew it would be a difficult night trying to capture some sleep, but it had been a very long day getting to this point, and I hoped that sleep would be mine, at least for a few hours.

Our early morning briefing came at 7:00 am. The commander who was running the recovery operation on Staten Island explained what we would be doing and the process involved. Everything from Manhattan was being loaded on dump trucks, then on barges, being carried across the river and to the Fresh Kill Landfill at Staten Island. We would be handling some security, and many of us would be actually looking through the rubble for personal items and remains of victims.

A visual of some of the debris field at Fresh Kill Landfill on Staten Island, where search and recovery operations were performed.

On the Staten Island ferry, our group was fully assembled and ready for the day's routine. We all had in our minds what we might be accomplishing that day. Little did we know what was in store for us at the landfill where all the debris from Manhattan was being taken for the sorting and inspection. As we walked gingerly across the deck of the ferry, coming towards us was a young mother with two young boys, probably around five and seven. They clung tightly to their mother, looking a bit intimidated by our five men in black. The mother wearing a flaring skirt and blouse and had an American flag draped around her shoulder and tucked neatly into her belt line. She and her sons walked straight up to me, suddenly stopped and she said, "My sons wanted to say thank you to you heroes who have come to help us." I was taken aback, quite frankly. Both her boys looked up at us, each smiling faintly, still clutching their mother's hands for reassurance.

I knelt down on one knee, looked at both boys, and said to them, "We are not the heroes here. You are. You are the heroes because you stayed. This is your home. You didn't run away. We came to see if we could help you and others like you here in these very difficult days." I stood up and looked at their mom, who was now beaming with delight that I had taken a moment to speak with her sons. "Good luck and Godspeed" she said to me as she walked away as briskly as she had appeared, her sons each giving a small wave as they departed.

Wow. How did this sixth generation farm boy, now funeral director and member of a sheriff's office, end up here? It was destined to be, and now I focused my mind as to what was to unfold in the days ahead, taking several deep breaths and pinching myself to make sure I wasn't rambling through a very bad dream. It was real, of course, and we packed into our suburban and headed for the landfill, the new home of all that was to come from Manhattan.

The next morning, our crew reported to our briefing. We were issued T-Vec, a full zippered white body suit with a front zipper, heavy gloves, tall rubber boots and a re-breather mask, all of which was intended to keep us safe and healthy as we went about our tasks, which were about to be assigned. We stood at the side of the open field as the front load tractors brought forward the piles of debris and neatly delivered them, completely covering the once barren field. As far as the eye could see, there was trash, broken glass, papers, steel, bricks, blocks, sinks, and, amongst it all, we knew there could be parts of some of those thousands who died just two weeks before in Manhattan. As about fifty of us stood at the side of the field surveying our work, the whistle blew, and everyone started the slow, methodical task of walking across the debris field, a shovel or rake in hand, to help separate the precious articles on the ground.

I was going forward on my hands and knees, and as I glanced up, saw no other person in a similar position. A majority of those searching were police and firemen. To my knowledge, that day I was probably the only one searching with any knowledge of the human anatomy, what it looked like, in whole and in part. If any recovery were to be made today, I knew in my heart it would be me doing the discovery. It was soon after that I made my first gruesome discovery: a human organ badly decomposed and unrecognizable in its disguise of dirt and grime. I motioned to the supervisor to bring me an evidence bag, and I encased the organ, labeled and initialed the date and time found. He shook his head in amazement that I could have found such amongst the debris field. While others walked from one side to the other, here I was on hands and knees, searching slowly, trying to find something that I prayed could be returned to a family member for closure. Again I asked myself, "What was I doing here?" God again had sent me on this mission, one of the most difficult in my almost three decades of dealing with death. My eyes welled up, my hands were shaking, but I knew I was here for a purpose, so I put on a fresh pair of latex gloves over my leathers and continued.

By day's end, we were all exhausted, mentally and physically. The suits were hot, you couldn't breathe, and the dirt and grime felt like it was two inches below your skin. Could we do this for another week? I was starting to question my own resolve, after only this very first day of recovery. I had been around, seen, smelled, recovered, embalmed, buried, exhumed and reburied death for so many years. Why was this so much different? These were innocent people, that's why. They didn't have a choice in their death that day in September. We would continue tomorrow, but right now, we needed to stop, for our own good.

The following days brought much of the same we had experienced in day one. We worked, conversed, slept and ate with volunteers from all over the United States: men and women from fire departments, volunteer ambulance corps, law enforcement, emergency responders. They were all here, from the biggest cities to the smallest towns, all pitching in to do their part in this huge recovery process. The last two days, for me, would be the most humbling. I was chosen with several others to work on the "conveyor belts." These were long thin conveyors running about sixty feet in length, starting at huge debris piles, running the sixty or so feet and up a steep incline, then re-dumping into a new debris pile at the very end. Our objective as "inspectors and grabbers" on the conveyor belt was to watch for specific items, grab what we could identify, and throw them to our right or left for further inspection. But what would we be looking for? Our answers came quickly.

Our morning meeting included members of the FAA and the NTSB, National transportation safety board. We were given a very detailed lesson on how to identify a piece or pieces that might have been part of the two airlines that entered the World Trade Center towers. We were instructed as to what to look for in type of aluminum used in the aircraft, paint colors, rivet patterns, wiring bundles, etc. It was important to retrieve as much of these aircrafts as possible; it was all evidence in what was the biggest crime scene ever on American soil.

After a couple hours of instruction, we were assigned our respective stations, and the signal was given to begin. The conveyors were moving quickly. The belts were each laden with all kinds of debris: concrete, glass, steel, wiring. The eyes had to scan the belt quickly as it came past you, and if you saw something that looked important, you had only seconds to pull it off and throw to the ground nearby. It would be inspected later.

I saw many pieces of aluminum. Yes, the aircraft colors were correct. The rivet patterns matched. The pull and throw process had begun. Two of my biggest recoveries were an aircraft window and part of the hydraulics of one of the plane's landing gear. The latter part almost took me with it as I grabbed it when it went by my station. It was all I could do to muster the strength to pull it from the conveyor and send it crashing to the earth below. And the aircraft window. What a strange feeling I had looking through it, knowing that just two weeks before, someone might have been sitting on the other side looking out, seeing the Twin Towers approaching them at over 400 miles per hour. I had recovered about thirty pieces of aircraft that day, some only a few inches in length or width. The largest was the part of the aircraft hydraulic system. I was exhausted, as much mentally as physically. The deed of taking down the Twin Towers was so huge, and the aftermath for thousands upon thousands of people, not only in this city, but literally around the world, was astounding. The whole event made one feel so small, so trivial, so irrelevant. Being there, digging through the rubble, helping the recovery effort, allowed one to at least try to find a place in one of the worst events in the history of mankind.

After six days, we packed out bags, got into our two unmarked sheriffs' cars and started the five hour road trip homeward. We were all quiet on the way home that day. All of us had in our own minds what we had experienced that week, what we had seen, smelled, touched, experienced. It was the most humbling experience I had ever encountered, being part of such a huge mass recovery. As the weeks and months went by, I thought frequently about my involvement there and about if what I had contributed really mattered at all. But, do any of us have an answer to that question at the end of a normal day or week, never mind a life-changing five days?

The two images engraved forever in my mind are standing at the base of an eighteen story rubble pile in Manhattan and being greeted by a sweet young lady wearing a flag accompanied by her two brave sons. I hope my efforts made a difference; I know they changed my life forever during a time that changed the world forever…

CHAPTER NINE

SOMEWHERE IN THE FREIGHT

The phone ringing in the middle of the night always meant someone had gone on, died, passed away, crossed over, sugared off. There were so many terms and descriptions for death. Young people would say "bit the dust". Older people were kinder and gentler, many liking the term "going on" or "slipping into the night." The verbage used really isn't significant. Whatever the term used, it all ends up the same. For the person for whom the bell tolls, there will be no morning oatmeal.

So it was 2:00 am and a hospital in Florida was telling me that Floyd so and so from our hometown had gone on to his last reward. As I struggled to force my eyelids to respond, a family member was put on the phone and instructed me that they wanted Floyd flown back to our town for just a local burial, no service, just a burial in the family plot next to Maude, his wife who had expired years before. I managed to write the information down, expressed my condolences to the family and hung up the

old clunky black telephone, a phone that actually had a bell in it. When it rang, you'd swear the dust would emerge from the curtains; it was that loud. I attempted to put cotton in the bells years before but got a brief, but powerful shock when I tried to open the bottom of the phone, its corporate insignia AT&T glaring at me on the warning that said, "Do not try to make adjustments to this phone." No kidding. I think the shock I received must have at stopped my fingernails from growing for at least six months.

As I stumbled groggily to my desk downstairs in the funeral home, my mind started to formulate a plan to retrieve the gentleman from Florida and bring him back here as his family had requested. I reviewed my funeral director yellow book, quickly discovering a funeral director in Florida near the hospital where Floyd had died. Perfect. Here's a guy who would retrieve Floyd and put him on an airliner to Rochester, the airport closest to me. I though more about it and decided to wait and call the funeral director at 7:00 am. There was no need of spoiling his night as well. I closed the yellow book, killed the light, and went back to bed. Unfortunately, my brain kept buzzing over the new death call, and a return to a restful sleep was not to be realized.

At 6:00 am, I was back at my desk dialing Florida and an undertaker who could assist me on that end. An answering service told me I had reached some corporate funeral home. The corporate guys always had answering services. The mom and pop guys usually lived on premises, like my wife and I, and were usually the sober voices that answered the phone.

"Of course," said the director in Florida. He would be very happy to claim Floyd, get the necessary paperwork and find an airliner going to Rochester within the next day or so.

The plan was set. There was an immediate family member locally who came in later that day, gave me the information I needed, selected a very humble pine casket and concrete grave liner, and paid in advance the amount I had estimated for all of the work, including the Florida undertaker and the airline fare. Life was good. Things always felt good when you had a plan in place and your family was pleased with their arrangements.

Twenty-four hours later I pulled the vehicle out of the garage, gassed it up, and headed north to Rochester, about ninety miles from our chapel. It would take me about an hour and forty five minutes to get to the airport. Then, after a quick drive to the freight office, which was only about 100 yards from the passenger gates, Floyd would be mine for the drive home.

In those days, the mid-1980s and before, there was little or no airport security. There was no TSA, few gates to show I.D's, etc. You just showed up, stated your business, and you were in. How innocent those days were. Little did we know how drastically things would change someday and how difficult simple things would become.

Arriving at the freight office after an uneventful trip, I skipped up the four steps into the office announcing my presence and my intentions. The guy behind the counter was munching on a tuna sandwich between swigs of soft drink and drags on a cigarette which almost choked me as I pulled back from him.

"Is flight 490 from Atlanta on time?" I queried. He looked at me half interested as he continued to devour the sandwich. "I have some remains on that flight coming to my funeral home from Florida."

With that, he wheeled around, pushed a button and looked at his TV screen. "It's already in," he proclaimed, "It came in early, about 20 minutes ago."

Fantastic! It was rare that a flight arrived early. This meant that I might even be home early. It was a nice day to drive, but wanting to get back out and beat the afternoon commuters made me smile.

"Back your car up to dock number 2 and we'll go fetch your guy," the attendant said.

I quickly signed the receipt for the airtray, which would contain the body, and I flew down the steps to await his next move.

My car was backed up, the rear door popped, and I stood in my blue shirt, tie and sport coat, awaiting the front loader- lift which should soon appear with my guy attached.

Instead, the same fellow came to the loading dock and started to say something, but his words were drowned out as an incoming airliner whined loudly overhead on its final approach and casted a shadow as it neared the runway just behind us.

"What's that?" I screamed, so I could be heard. "I didn't hear you."

The attendant had a sheepish look on his face as he jumped down and stood eyeball to eyeball with me next to the rear bumper.

"I can't find your guy. I know he's here. I just can't find him"

My mind was now processing this information. You can't find my guy. A dead man in a standard pine and cardboard box, the size of a casket with stickers all over it saying "human remains", "handle with care", airline logos, etc., and this guy is telling me he's misplaced him? This isn't your standard shipment of copy paper, carpet remnants, or plastic actions figures. This is a deceased human we're talking about. You just don't misplace human remains.

I had to cut the cold veil of silence by asking, "You didn't give him to somebody by accident did you?"

He looked at me like I thought he was a moron. I think the term "moron" went through both of our skulls at the same time.

"We'll turn the place over. We'll find him. I know he's here," the attendant tried to reassure me.

I sat on the bumper of the car as he re-entered the building. Five minutes turned to ten, ten to fifteen. Finally, the tractor emerged with my guy's airtray on the front, the driver smiling gleefully.

"Some guy threw a tarp over the box out back. Sorry for the wait."

We loaded Floyd, I headed the car south, and we returned to the chapel unscathed. The next day I buried Floyd with a simple grave side prayer, and we called it a day.

44

The ironic part of the story was that just at the end of the service, the family member told me how great it was that Floyd was now home and tucked away with his family.

They said he had had a very frightful time once as a kid when he was lost in the woods for a couple of days. Wow. Floyd had almost done it again. Sleep well Floyd; you can't get lost again.

CHAPTER TEN

FILLING A GRAVE: A FAMILY TRADITION

It had been a long day. The traditional calling hours had been very busy with a constant stream of people going up the front steps, through the front door, signing the register book and in to visit with the family. And then there were the kids. How could all of these kids belong to one family? Had a school bus stopped out front and discharged the extras just to make me more anxious as the youngsters scooted in and out of the old crowd, me holding my breath as they skipped among the aged, many barely in command of canes and crutches. Youngsters in funeral homes are welcome but always make me nervous as they run and jump through the crowd. I am sure that at any moment an elderly person will go flying, cane in one direction, false teeth and hat in another!

But today, luck was with us. We had a few close calls but no spills, bumps, or bruises. The minister had said his part, the family had each gone to the casket to say their goodbyes, and I at last was in possession, at least for a second, of a few moments of silence in the funeral home as I made the final preparations for the trip to the cemetery which was just a short eight miles away. As I took one last glance at the gentlemen to be buried and reviewed my list of what was to be buried with him and what was to be saved, a tug on my coat from behind brought me back to reality.

"Hey, mister. Are we taking grandpa to his new place now?" came the inquiry from a young man who couldn't be more than seven or eight.

I told him to go out with the rest of the family, and I would be bringing grandpa right along. I had no idea that this little boy would soon be helping me do my job.

It was hot that day, pushing 90 I guessed, and as I glanced at my watch, it was just past 3:00 pm. We were in good shape. The trip to the cemetery would take about fifteen to twenty minutes, figuring on the usual procession speed of 45 mph or so. You never wanted to drive too fast out of respect for the deceased, but you also didn't want to drive too slow because people do not like following funeral processions. They get anxious, nervous, and sometimes angry, and from time to time will try to pass a line of cars even in the most precarious of situations on the highway.

Within minutes, we had loaded grandpa in the back of the hearse.

The flowers designated for the cemetery were loaded in the car, and what looked like fifteen to twenty cars were lined up behind us as we headed around the corner and out of the village limits. The minister in the front seat with me in the lead car was looking quickly through his notes. I wondered how long his graveside service would be, mainly because of the heat. Would he look at his followers under the tent and decide to do the short version? We would soon find out.

As the procession wheeled out of town, the heat was searing. It came off the pavement in waves as we made our way east, slowly meandering by the Catholic cemetery in town and then on the main road to our destination. The minister chatted about the heat and how he and his wife would be going to the mountains over the weekend to fish. He was hoping the fishing would be good and the mosquito count down, but he wasn't optimistic. His voice gave him away. I checked my dash. All looked good: fuel , temperature, oil pressure. This was the kind of a day you didn't want to break down on.

Within a short ten minutes, we turned into the cemetery. This was an older cemetery with probably less than a hundred graves total. The vault was in the ground, the tent was set, and the vault man

48

stood near the grave looking very exhausted and near heat stroke. His blue shirt showed the wetness of his toil to prepare things for what I hoped would be a quick prayer. The casket was situated on the placer over the grave; the family sat and stood nearby, and I nodded to the minister to begin as he wiped his brow and juggled the bible and suit coat from one hand to the other. It was still scorching hot. Fortunately, the prayers were brief, the blessings given, and I concluding by thanking everyone for attending, asking them to be careful in their departure.

Suddenly, one of the sons came up to me grabbed my arm and said, "Mr. Swan... you've worked way too hard for us today. We want you to set a spell and just let us finish things up for you."

He led me by the arm to a small stone marker about 24 inches high and had me sit. I wasn't quite sure of what was to come, but the vault man looked at me and shook his head, his bewilderment close to mine in its degree. The tent came down quickly and was stowed, and there it was, the open grave, waiting for the cement cover to be lowered onto the vault. The casket had already been lowered to its final resting place. What followed next was truly noteworthy. The man who had made me sit down gave a whistle that would have stopped Marilyn Monroe. From the back of the lineup of cars rolled an old jeep with at least eight youngsters of all ages crammed into it. They all piled out with shovels, picks, and rakes. Several started swinging from the back of the vault truck and its block and tackle system as others started throwing dirt into the grave like it was an Olympic event.

"Been a tradition for years," said the son to me. "We've always covered up our own".

I sat looking, sweating, and praying. "Please," I thought, "Don't let anyone get hurt doing this traditional thing."

Forty minutes passed. The dirt continued to fly. The clothes the kids were wearing were completely black, but they were smiling like it was a day off from school. When the tradition was finished, I packed up the minister, and we headed home.

He turned and said to me, "Does that happen often?"

I laughed. "Often?" I said, "It's a once in a lifetime deal, pun intended."

CHAPTER ELEVEN
READING OF THE WILL

The service had gone as planned, the procession to the cemetery was uneventful, and now the family walked around the grave chatting with one another and those who had come from afar to bury Regina. She had been a nurse and worked her entire life in a big eastern city. Never taking a husband and producing no family, Regina was now at repose in her simple wood casket, which currently sat on the lowering device waiting to be put in the cement vault which was already in the ground. What a strange tradition this burial business is, when you think about it. We embalm people with chemicals, dress them, put more chemicals in the form of makeup and hairspray on them, then place them in a casket and encrypt that in concrete or steel. We go through so much ritual, only to return to the dirt from which we came. It is a strange custom indeed, but we've been performing the same ritual since the time of the Egyptians and even before, so we give it little thought.

The sun was waning in the late afternoon sky, as the mourners now stood near their cars readying to depart from the cemetery. The man who had dug the grave was also ready to go to work, his pickup truck tucked behind the little storage shed nearby. A puff of blue smoke told me his pipe was lit, and he was staging near his equipment and would be ready to go as soon as the casket was lowered. A gentleman in a neatly pressed blue suit approached me from my left, gingerly stepping around a headstone in order to get to my location.

"Excuse me," he said. "I know this is probably an unusual request, but what is actually left of our family is here today, and we were wondering if we might be able to go back to your funeral home to read the will."

This indeed was an odd request. A family had never asked such before, so I was kind of surprised, yet also delighted. If a will was to be read, that meant the finances should be settled quickly and that would insure the funeral bill might get paid post haste! I pondered a quick moment. What did Regina have? Who would get what? This might be an interesting end to what started out as a very typical day of funeralizing! With no family, she had worked hard all her life in the metropolis, and I assume she had some pretty high living expenses there. Her funeral was rather meager because, when the family was making arrangements, they had no idea how much money Regina actually had, and so they chose a very simple funeral for her.

"I'd be more than happy to have you folks come back to the funeral home," I said to the man in the blue suit.

His smile, on a very rounded face, told me he was indeed pleased, and he turned to the meager crowd of twelve and announced, "Let's all go back to the funeral home folks. Mr. Ramsey, Regina's attorney, is going to read the will. Then we can all head home before dark."

Without further delay, the mourners got into their vehicles and headed out under the antique wrought iron gate that hung over the main entrance, the same wrought iron gate that had been passed under after dozens, maybe even hundred, of funerals. The funeral parlor was only about six country blocks from the cemetery, and the cars arrived out front very quickly, their occupants scurrying up the sidewalk and into the front door. I went to the chapel without delay, put out the register stand with the microphone attached, and re-positioned some chairs within a few feet of where the attorney would hopefully please everyone with his recitation.

The man in the blue suit cleared his throat and nodded to Mr. Ramsey to begin. Ramsey, an older gentleman, approached the

52

podium, unbuttoned his fish bone coat and reached into his left inner pocket to remove a faded yellow envelope. The envelope looked as ancient as the sport coat, only it did not show any signs of ash burns, like the sport coat did. Was he a cigarette or pipe smoker? Pipe, I presumed. As he passed me, I detected a brief odor of what could have been very fine cherry blend. Ramsey proceeded to remove from the other coat pocket an ancient pair of half-moon reading glasses. He plopped them on the end of his bulbous nose as he snapped the yellow parchment open with a quick flip of the left wrist. And so he began all the legalese of being of right mind and not of any duress and of sound body and so on and so on. I thought, almost out loud, "Come on, get to the good stuff. Daylight is wasting."

Ramsey paused a moment in order to get everyone's full attention, then he began the giveaway: "To my loyal cat, Scarsdale, who has been with me continuously for the past ten years, I leave the amount of $75,000."

The twelve family members sitting in attendance gasped collectively. It was an inhalation so deep that I thought for sure all of the dust in the room would instantaneously get sucked into their open mouths. One older woman in the front row in a purple hat and shawl started fanning herself from left to right to get some air. Her color had quickly gone from rosy to pale.

Ramsey continued, "To my trustworthy dog, Randolph, I leave the amount of $125,000."

There was no breath this time. A couple of the folks started coughing instead, their throats tightening. So far, Regina had left $200,000 to her animals. Would there be more? I stood at the front door thinking, "Gee, I just buried this lady pretty much as a pauper. Think I could get them to rethink the merchandise?"

I didn't know if the grave was yet filled. Maybe we could upgrade that casket to a nice oak or cherry. It was a fleeting thought only, born from the disparity between how Regina was buried and how much money she had. I was happy to have served the family.

Money really does not mean anything when you are in the cemetery: the place where men and women really are equal, the place where everyone is the same.

Ramsey continued with the reading of Regina's will. She left a few more thousand to this society and that church. A couple of the people in attendance did get her old Cadillac, but the bulk of Regina's money went to her loyal pets. The creatures who were with her daily and possibly the only ones in her life who didn't ask for anything but to be fed and to be loved, were the ones who got the most. They gave love, loyalty, and companionship in return for the same.

Within minutes, Regina's only living relatives were down the sidewalk, into their cars, and headed east to that big apple on the coast. Regina was at her last stop, in her town where she had been born, her worldy possessions distributed, and now those recipients were starting the cycle all over again, except for her cat and dog, who couldn't leave anything material behind. As I closed the front door, I couldn't help but think what an odd day it had been. And in the chapel, there was still that slight hint of Ramsey's cherry blend that would forever remind me of that day and that woman who valued her animals more than her relatives, probably because her pets gave her more of what money can't buy.

CHAPTER TWELVE

A BLACK CAT IN OCTOBER

It was a terrific fall day in mid-October. The sky was brilliant blue, and white rolling clouds raced from west to east as the afternoon's late day sun moved to make its exit over the crimson maple tree out front. The afternoon's calling hours had gone quite well, and a good number of people had shown up to pay their respects to the current occupant of the reposing room. It was my usual practice to be at the front door to open and close, greet people as they entered, asking for their wraps when appropriate, and to point out the register stand which would accept their signature for the family. And so the afternoon was gone. The family had left the funeral home; now it was time to pick up, run the vacuum, check the restroom, check the deceased, yes, check the deceased. It was not unusual that during calling hours, visitors would place things in the casket or even on the deceased. Those items could range from notes, to playing cards, to more bizarre items. Once, years before, I had found a note, wide open, telling the deceased that he still owed the visitor some money, but not to worry about it! That note was folded and neatly tucked into the man's suit. The family wouldn't need to be aware of that one. I learned several years before to expect almost anything at any time, and that was the rule in funeral service.

The brief two hour break between the afternoon and evening sets of calling hours really wasn't lengthy enough for any time to rest. A quick bite to eat, quicker shave and perhaps a clean shirt, and it was back at the front door, ready to greet the family as they returned for the evening calling hours. The porch, step and sidewalk lights were all lit and generated a warm glow, leading from the street to the funeral home entrance. A brief wind gust blew autumn leaves across the walkway as the family entered and went into the parlor to await the evening's visitors. Evenings were usually quite busy at the funeral home. People were done with work, had had dinner and were accustomed to visit, view the deceased, and sign the register book. It was tradition, tradition that had gone on for decades in small towns and cities all over the country.

As I stood at the entrance chatting with an old friend, I looked out the front door and saw a black cat making its way up the sidewalk. His devilish eyes shined from the walkway lights as he swaggered his way up the sidewalk, up the four steps and to the front door. He paused. I opened the door to step out, but before I could, he stepped in! Not stopping, the cat made a quick left, walked past the register stand and straight toward the casket and family about twelve yards ahead. Those sitting in chairs stopped chatting, their eyes pulled to the feline, as he made his way into the front room. The guest never stopped, went to the casket, did a U-turn, walked back out the exact same path, exited the funeral home, and meandered down the walkway.

My friend Kenney asked, "Friend of yours?"

"Never saw the beast before," I said.

It was October, Halloween was just around the corner, and a black cat visited the local funeral parlor. It kind of all fit together very appropriately, I thought. We were only missing a thunder and lightning storm, but we'll save that for another time. And I had made one error with that October evening visitor: I failed to get him or her to sign the register book.

CHAPTER THIRTEEN
COME IN OUT OF THE STORM...

The morning of the funeral, I awoke very anxious. I had listened to the wind blow most of the night. It was bone chillingly cold. As I looked out the venetian blind from my bed at daylight, I could see it still snowing, heavy and still piling up. We must have gotten a good six or eight inches overnight. The sidewalks would have to be cleared early, the lead car shoveled out and warmed up. The man with the hearse we rented would be coming from about eight miles away. I wasn't worried though; he was always there on time and ready to go.

John, the fellow whose mom I was burying that day was a likable cuss. He was always throwing his hand in the air when you would see him and giving a big "Hi." He would be taking over the family farm now that his mom and dad were gone. He had a couple of horses and a mule or two. I'm not sure which job he spent the most time with, as he worked away from town every day.

The phone rang shortly after eight that morning, and John informed me that he had the road cleared, and we were good to come to the house with my lead car and the hearse. He said there would be maybe five or six other family cars driving up for the prayers before we headed down to church. I felt better knowing the road was at least passable, but I was still anxious, the snow continuing to build and swirl as my lead car and hearse lurched through the white maze heading up the hill to gather the casket and family.

Usually a procession with a lead car, hearse, and family vehicles is a very stoic, dignified and reverent event. But that morning, that procession would be interrupted briefly by a once in a life time event.

We had secured the casket in the hearse, loaded a few flower pieces around it and readied to make our way down the hill to church. The snow was coming down harder now, and, as John jumped in the front seat next to me, we looked at each other briefly, each almost covered in the new white stuff after only being out a few minutes readying to come down the hill. He had one of those big furry hats on with the ear flaps pulled own around his cheeks. John's hat was not really the fashion that one would normally wear to church, but today was winter times ten, and it seemed appropriate, so I just smiled as I looked at him, and we started our downward spiral from the house. Behind us, followed about six cars, lights on bright, but dimmed significantly by the steady downward blowing of new snow.

About twenty yards from the house, John put his left hand out and said to me, "Stop for just a second."

I wondered if he had forgotten something at the house that he wanted to run back and retrieve? I would soon have my question answered.

We were about twenty yards or so from a barn that was within ear shot of the house we had just departed from. Near the barn, you could barely make out two animals, looking like four legged statues standing in the storm. John opened the car door, stepped out into the blowing mass, the snow pelting him hard and fast. He raised his hands to his face and yelled out as loud as he could "Daniel, Billy, get your asses down here and get in the barn."

I bit my lip so I wouldn't laugh out loud, but it was too late. The scene didn't feel real: a funeral procession in the dead of winter, stopped by a family member to order his animals in to feed. When John re-entered the car, he saw me smiling and started laughing himself. He made a comment or two about how stupid animals can be from time to time. We proceeded to church, then to the cemetery.

As I placed flowers on his mom's grave that evening just before dark, I reflected again about what an unusual day it had been. Today's work was done. The snow removal would start tomorrow, and I would be reminded of those wandering farm animals as I cleared today's snow and every snowfall to follow.

CHAPTER FOURTEEN

A STORY MADE FOR THUNDERSTORMS

There have been few times that I have actually witnessed something remarkable in the funeral business. Over the decades, I have been questioned by so many people who asked such things as, "Have you ever seen a body sit up?" or "Have you ever seen a ghost in the funeral home while at work or during an overnight thunderstorm?"

The simple answer is no. These things are pretty much urban legends, passed on from generation to generation, and are subjects made into third rate or less TV movies. Funeral homes have always been the subject of potential scary movies made for kids. It's just natural I suppose. You have some caskets, many times a body in a preparation room, and always, always, the wind blowing, maybe a little thunder and lightning thrown in, all a recipe for some good late night TV.

But one day, in broad daylight, I did experience an event which I would deem to be just a bit out of the ordinary. It was late afternoon at the funeral home. A gal in her forties, dressed smartly in a business suit, entered the funeral home unannounced and walked to my cherry desk where I was seated. She placed in front of me a box I assumed to be cardboard, wrapped in brown paper with a string surrounding its perimeter.

"These are my mother's ashes," she blurted. "They are in a vase which broke by itself, allowing her to seep out onto the shelf where I had the vase sitting."

OK. This was going to be interesting. We exchanged pleasantries for a moment. She gave me the details of her mother's passing several years ago, and how it was decided to keep the urn, not vase, at home instead of being buried. She went on to tell me that as she sat in silence one day at home reading a book, she heard what she described as someone running a fingernail over a chalkboard. She said it was very unusual, as there was no one else in the room, and there was no electronic media.

Turning around to where the sound came from, she looked up and saw her mother's urn in its usual place, but something around it seemed to suggest movement of some type. She arose from her chair and approached the urn. When she came within a foot of the urn, she noticed a crack from the midline to the top of the urn, and more disturbing, a small stream of ash that was seeping out of the crack and onto the shelf itself. As she told me the story, I was trying to diagnose her comments and look for anything in her demeanor that would give me reason to doubt her narrative.

"I wanted you to examine the vase, if you would, and give me your impressions of what could have caused this to happen," she said.

"And has anything unusual happened since that day?" I asked her.

She shook her head no.

I reached over to the box, undid the aged yellowed string, and undid the outer paper wrapping, giving way to a brown box, which also showed some age. Standing up, I undid the flaps of the box, reached down and extracted the urn, which was dark violet in color and sporting a swirl of some design which was not painted on, but rather part of the glass blowing process, I assumed.

Sitting the urn on the table squarely in front of her and only twenty inches or so from my vantage point, I did see some paper tape of some sort had been adhered to the glass from the midpoint to the top. She pointed to the tape with a well- manicured nail and said, "I taped it to keep any more ash from coming out."

"What would have caused that?" she queried.

It was an older urn I explained, not purchased from us. After some questioning, I discovered that her Mom had died more than fifteen years ago, and the urn had sat in the same place since her death.

"I only dust around it," she said, "but really haven't moved it in years. I was always afraid I'd break it, and that would be horrible."

I had no answers for her. The urn looked pretty normal. There was no indication that it had been mishandled in any way. I really couldn't explain why it had happened to her.

I asked her if she wanted to purchase a new urn, to which I could transfer the cremains into, but she declined.

"No, I'll take her home with me, and think about maybe scattering her ashes in the next year or so. She has been with me a long time now."

At that moment, the phone rang, and I had to excuse myself into the next room to take the call. When I returned, the gal was now standing and had retreated a couple of feet from her chair. As I approached her, I saw that her right hand was raised over her mouth, a startled look on her face. I looked at the urn, still in the same position which I had placed it. There were very minute traces of ash now seeping out from the tape and onto the top of the cherry table.

"Mother was an avid traveler during her life," the woman remarked, "Maybe she just doesn't have it our of her system."

I wrapped the urn in plastic, placed it back in the box, and the woman retreated out the door as quickly as she had entered. I never heard from her or saw her again. Was her story true? I had no reason to doubt her. Some things you just can't explain. You just have to save them for stories to be told during a late night thunderstorm...

CHAPTER FIFTEEN
A HOMICIDE, SUICIDE OR SO IT SEEMED...

It was a late day in fall. The maples that stood around the funeral home had started shedding their leaves, and the caretaker of the local Masonic lodge was making his way down the sidewalk with rake in hand, presumably to start the task of the yearly leaf gather. The lodge, a great old two story brick building, was just a block from our business and the home to at least two dozen members of the fraternity that gathered every other Monday evening. I had often thought the lodge would have made a wonderful funeral home. It had a full kitchen and gathering area downstairs and a wide chamber upstairs where their meetings were held. There was beautiful wood work, hardwood floors and tall long windows, the kind not found in todays' buildings, magnificent but surely huge heat losses.

My portable phone which I had with me when I was outside working blatted out a couple of rings before I could dislodge it from my fall hooded sweatshirt. On the other end, a man identified himself as a lieutenant with the state police and asked me to meet him and one of the local coroners at an address just across town. It was maybe three blocks at most. I knew the corner the house was sitting on and could almost visualize the house as I ran up the front steps and inside to change my clothes. I had often marveled at my ability to shed outside work clothes and put on a dress pair of slacks, long sleeve dress shirt, black tie shoes, and sometimes a neck tie, all within the matter of two minutes or less. And Superman thought he was good.

As I dashed out the back door to my removal car, which was a black Chevy Suburban with tinted windows, I did a quick visual to make sure my removal cot was tucked in the back and ready to go: it was. Out the driveway, down the street, and across Main Street, I steered the big vehicle to the street number the trooper had given me. A I neared the house, I could see at least two trooper cars in place, the local p.d. car nearby, and a couple of volunteer firemen standing near. There were no red lights, no rushing people; everything was just kind of subdued and laid back. This was a death scene.

I rolled down the window of my Suburban as I wheeled into the cinder driveway. A trooper nearly half as big as the house looked down at me and asked, "You the local guy?" Now did he say "loco" or "local"? There is a distinct difference, especially in this kind of situation.

"I'm Stan, the local funeral director. I was told to show up. I believe the coroner is on the way. What's up?"

"It's not a pretty scene," replied the trooper. "Gun involved, at least two victims found so far. Think you can drive up pretty close to the front door." With that, he stepped back, his large pale grey trooper hat allowing the morning sun to hit me square on as I cocked my head to the right searching for the rest of my approach.

As I ran up the two short front steps to the front door, I was met by a member of the local criminal investigation team, part of the local trooper barracks. His long black coat looked a size too small and was hardly enough to conceal his sidearm, which was neatly nestled into a small holster on his hip.

"Don't touch anything, and you're going to need some help," he said as he motioned to another trooper positioned on the steps. I quickly entered the house, not wanting to have a conversation with the man, just wanting to see what I was going to be dealing with. Immediately in front of me in a narrow hallway lay a female, face down, in shirt and jeans, also wearing some type of flip flop shoes.

She was of average weight and height, but I could not determine the age from the rear angle from which I viewed.

"She's a local gal we think," said the investigator, now just inches behind me and making me feel quite uncomfortable. "Looks like a single shot to the chest. The boyfriend, well maybe acquaintance, is in the bedroom, also a single gunshot, looks self-inflicted."

Now this was most interesting. It was very, very rare that our small town had a homicide and/or apparent suicide. It just didn't happen here. Everyone knew each other, most everyone got along with one another, and this just didn't fit the realm of our *Leave it to Beaver* community. But, here it was, and I was standing in the middle of it waiting for instruction. Just as the investigator finished briefing me, another man exited the bedroom. This was a different coroner than I usually had dealt with, but his face was familiar.

"They'll both have to go to Rochester," he replied. "We've already made ID and contacted the families. The girl will be yours when the autopsies are done."

What that meant was the family had already selected our funeral home to take care of their daughter. I looked at the name. Yes, I knew the family. They were in business locally, a nice couple, and this they would have an extremely hard time dealing with.

I returned to my vehicle, removed my stretcher and gingerly rolled it up the old sidewalk, which had not seen any repair in a number of years. When I entered the home, the coroner stopped and conferred with me as to how we would make the removal of the two victims we had on the scene. We lowered the stretcher to the floor, near the foot of the female victim, placed a sheet on the floor, and, with the assistance of the investigator, rolled her over on the the sheet. The investigator paused after the first move to take a couple more photographs and take notes as we worked. Soon, she was in my cot and ready for transport, and we removed her and placed her in my vehicle for the trip to the medical examiner's. The coroner then asked me if I would assist him with the second victim, a male who was in the bedroom. The coroner would be taking him to the medical examiner, as well, for autopsy. We entered the bedroom through another door at the far north of the hallway, and there the other body was, barely lying prone on the bed, his arms flared out, a shotgun within a foot or two of the victim and copious amounts of blood and tissue surrounding him. Death surely was instant for this fellow. The gun has always been what seems to be a first choice for those who want a quick exit.

With a little more effort and substantially more equipment and personal protective gear (gown, shoe covers, and heavier gloves), we were soon able to remove the second victim, placing him directly into a disaster pouch: a heavy rubber zippered bag made especially for difficult trauma or burn victims. He was soon loaded back into the vehicle of the coroner and was on his way to autopsy, ninety miles to the north of our small town. After conferring with the detectives and receiving some family notification numbers for the victim in my possession, I jumped into my car and headed for the funeral home. A short stop there, then I would also to head north to the city. I dreaded the task of the next few hours. Talking with the parents of the woman would be difficult. I had known them both for many, many years. It was, I knew, going to be gut wrenching for them to hear the story of what had happened to their daughter that day. But I would let the detectives make the notification; that was their job. Mine would come in the next couple of days when I would have to sit with the victim's parents and arrange for her final disposition.

Life is so fragile, so fluid, changing at a moment's notice from calm and collected to violent and tragic. Homicide and suicide are an hourly occurrence in America, but they take a little extra wind out of your sails when they are in your own little town.

CHAPTER SIXTEEN
A SLIPPERY SLOPE

The weather had been pretty foul overnight. Heavy rain and wind had produced a good crop of debris for me to sweep from the entrance ways. Looking Eastward, I could see a faint glimmer of daybreak, but the sky looked threatening still. It didn't appear that it would clear at all anytime soon. I picked up the morning paper. Thank goodness it had been wrapped in plastic, or it wouldn't have been acceptable even for the birdcage. But alas, there wasn't much daily content in it to look at anyway.

The morning hours flew by quickly, and I made my way through the daily routine of catching up. In the funeral business, you are always catching up. There are always more papers to complete, stock to relook at, phone calls to make. You are really never done. You just try to keep ahead of the game if you can. I was just trying to keep one step ahead.

It was mid morning when the office door opened, and a middle aged heavy set gentleman appeared, walking quickly to me and uttering a garbled "good morning". I hurriedly seated the man in an overstuffed chair and swiftly sat next to him to inquire of how I might be of help to him.

"My wife is not all that well young man, and I'd like to talk to you about future services for her if I could. She wants to be cremated."

I immediately knew what he wanted, so I grabbed a file and started taking notes from his, getting his wife's biographical information, survivors list, etc. As I asked him questions about his wife, he would ponder on the answers, chuckle quite a bit and tell me brief stories about how he and she had met, romanced, broke down in the Ozark mountains and so on. We had a delightful conversation, and I knew right off that he had taken a liking to me as he started asking about myself, how I ended up as an undertaker, where I was from and so on.

After about twenty minutes of somewhat light conversation we started to talk about the costs associated with cremating his wife. As I reviewed the cost involved for the immediate cremation, we finally arrived at the subject of the rigid container which she would have to be placed in to go into the cremation unit itself for the process. I told him, "This container is made of re-enforced cardboard, with light plywood framework and costs $245.00."

He looked at me and said, "Gee Stan, that's a little steep for just a cardboard box that's going to be burned up in a couple of hours. Do you have anything less expensive?"

He had kind of a sheepish grin on his face, perhaps a bit embarrassed about asking for something less, and I immediately blurted out without ever considering what I was doing and said, "Yes, but it has Chiquita stamped all over it."

There was less than a micro second of silence, but then he started belly laughing so hard I thought he was going to burst. His face arrived at bright red, and his eyes were wet . I couldn't help myself; the laughter was contagious. I thought, "I may have made a critical error here, joking with a man I barely knew."

After a minute or so, he said to me, "I'll think we'll go with the first choice. She really wasn't a fruit person," and he continued to chuckle for another minute or so. Within another five minutes, we had completed our agreement for what he had selected for his wife. As quickly as he had arrived, he was up and at the door, ready to make his exit. Turning to me he said, "Stan, it's been my pleasure to meet you, and I appreciate all the advance help you have given me. I know I've come to the right place. I'll let you know how things go for me and the Mrs."

As I closed the door and turned toward the office, our office gal, Friday, poked her head into the room and said, "We have a new death call." There was no time to soak in all that had just transpired. Now, it was time to drive into a new call and think about a new family to serve. It might turn into another day with no lunch. Maybe I will at least have time for a quick banana…

CHAPTER SEVENTEEN
THE RECOVERY AT KATRINA

Hurricane Katrina was the most destructive Atlantic storm of the 2005 hurricane season. The seventh most deadly Atlantic storm ever recorded, Katrina took at least 1,833 lives during the storm and the subsequent flooding. It did four times the damage of Hurricane Andrew in 1992, and its effects upon Mississippi and Louisiana were catastrophic. Homes, businesses, beaches, levees, and even cemeteries were taken by this monster storm, debris ending up as far as twelve miles inland.

As part of a national recovery team, I spent almost two weeks in the area of Biloxi and Gulfport aiding in the recovery and identification of many of Katrina's victims. This is that story as recorded in the daily journal that I was able to make notes in, many times in the light of a flashlight or similar device. This search and recovery was massive, using the talents of thousands of citizens with special skills from police to forensics to volunteers, all with the same goal in sight: trying to find, identify and return victims to their families. Unfortunately, many people were never recovered. Huge numbers were either swept out to sea or buried in mud and debris and have yet to be found.

Years after Katrina, partial remains of victims are still being recovered, and much like the terror attack in New York City, the gathering of remains and personal effects goes on. Those living there continue to deal with the storm and tragedy that was Katrina. I salute their courage and determination as they continue to try to put their lives back in order after that terrible week in August of 2005. I am honored to have been part of the recovery process.

It was on Friday, Sept. 2nd that our actual orders were processed, and we were told to report to Anaston, Alabama and the Noble Training Center, part of the huge complex that is Fort McClellan. My flight from Rochester NY was quite uneventful; however, it was super busy as it was Labor Day weekend, and it seemed everyone was going somewhere. Our operations would be directed by FEMA: they called the shots on movement of people, materials, etc. Once we were in place, our first concerns getting into the "war zone", as I will call it, was fuel. In most areas that we were traveling to, the power was out, so the filling stations were all closed.

Our first orders were to load our government vehicles and motor to Biloxi, an area that was hit extremely hard. There were already National Guard and ICE officers (Immigration Custom and Enforcement) on the ground there. These agencies and equipment had been sent in by the appropriate governors of Mississippi and Louisiana, as they feared large amounts of looting would take place. One has to understand that this area had just stopped existing. People were sitting on curbs; phone and telephone poles were down; water was running out of broken water mains; there was mud, silt and flood debris everywhere you looked; stray dogs looked through garbage cans trying to scavenge something to eat. It was like watching a bad movie on late night TV, yet here it was in our own country. This wasn't a third world country. This was the Gulf coast, one of the most beautiful areas of the country, now in ruins.

Our nine vehicles were loaded with supplies, MRE's (meals ready to eat), bottled water, medical supplies, and 1600 sheets for our portable morgue that would be set up at our destination. We had everything needed to self-sustain our work in the field for at least ten days. But we were only in Biloxi for a short time before our orders changed, and we were told to go to Gulfport, now deemed the hardest hit. It was a six hour drive, so we set our vehicles in motion, pondering all the way what our next experiences would be when we arrived there. We were told to call our OPS center every two hours so they would know where we were and if we were safe. We had no weapons on us, just our ingenuity and determination in purpose, but that wouldn't save us if we got involved in some ugly incident along the way. So onward we drove down Rt. 20 to Birmingham to Meridian then into Gulfport, Mississippi. Along the way, we were fueled at stations that had been taken over by the Guard. Signs at the stations said "FOR EMERGENCY / RELIEF AGENCIES ONLY." If you were just a member of the traveling public, you wouldn't be fueling there; you were out of luck. A lot of people were out of luck. We traveled 420 miles that day before getting to our final "jumping off" point. Here we would be camping out, literally, doing our work in recovery and identification. In Gulfport, we were put on the Keesler Air Force base. In a partially destroyed hangar, we would be setting up all of our morgue equipment that had arrived before we did: everything from photography to x-ray and personal protective gear, and I was told a body bag supply of 5,000 in number.

Our first introduction to "roughing it" was when we were shown the giant reefer trucks where we were to sleep. Each truck had twenty four berths, or bunks, built into the back made of two by fours and plywood; that was it. One built in air conditioner at the front of the truck was supposed to keep us cooled down a bit from the expected high temperatures of ninety to one hundred degrees that we were told to expect. Before the actual man made latrines arrived, we went out into the field, walked over several wooden planks and stood or squatted, whatever our need was, and relieved ourselves into a six foot deep pit that had been entrenched just for us. As we peered out from the hangar in which we were to accomplish our work, we could see several other refrigerated trucks already lined up, side by side. We were told there were at least one hundred bodies already inside, awaiting our processing and identification.

After a very uncomfortable first night in the temporary housing, we had our first briefing at 7:00 the next morning. We were instructed that we would be working from ten am to six pm, depending on the number of deceased being brought in. The big concern was for our safety. Working in very hot temperatures, we were told to be constantly taking fluids, as we would be in full protective garb, white zippered suits, head protective gear, masks and gloves. All of this equipment would hold heat and would tend to raise the body temperature as we did the day's work. So our crew went to work for the day. There would be five or six people actually working in the rear of the trailers, re-arranging, removing and replacing body bags with victims of the hurricane. Once a new body arrived, it would be tagged and numbered, placed in the trailer and put on the schedule for processing.

The damaged hangar at Gulfport where our receiving and identification tents were set up to process Katrina storm victims.

There were nine different stations that a deceased would be scrutinized through, including initial photography, to gathering of any personal effects, fingerprinting, x-ray, DNA sample gathering, and so on. One person would stay with that particular body through the whole process, accompanying the gurney from point one to point nine, gathering the paperwork as it made its way through, then re-introduce the remains to the refrigerated trucks. We could process from a dozen to fifteen people a day, and we would take a break from time to time to re-hydrate, change gloves, etc.

The high point of the second day, and we really needed a high point, was when we heard President Bush would be coming to Gulfport. We had hoped to catch a sight of him, but it didn't happen. We did watch Air Force One as it came into land that day; it taxied to the other side of the base and the President was whisked away, never to come near our side of the operation. I mean really, who wants to visit a place where human remains are being handled, stored and identified?

One of the more interesting segments of the remains movement was that we were getting bodies brought in that had been washed out of cemeteries. Caskets had been sucked out of the ground and out of above ground mausoleums by the height and pressure of the wave that had gone through Gulfport. Many of the cemetery remains that were brought in were fully dressed in suits and dresses, embalmed and in their "repose" state of lying in a casket. We were told to put those remains aside; they were not a priority. "New victims" needed to be identified and returned to their families first.

One gentleman I talked to survived the twenty-two foot wave by luckily being in the second floor window of his mother in-laws apartment.

"You had an interesting night?" I inquired of him. The black man flashed a big smile at me, and I saw that his front tooth had a gold star implant which was quite remarkable.

"Indeed Mr., indeed. I though sure I was a goner, but the Good Lord was there to watch for me, that's for sure."

The parking lot of that particular building which the man was in had stacks and rows of cars that had been swept together like tiny hot wheels, all scrunched together and completely destroyed.

The heat of the work every day was almost unbearable. Temperatures that reached the high nineties and even one hundred took their toll on the staff and equipment. Two one hundred twenty kilowatt generators were burned out over a forty eight hour period, trying to keep the equipment and huge fans operating. After a few days in the reefers, we managed to have some huge tents set up for us to crash in at the end of the day. They were a sweet relief from being in the back of a truck, and we all settled into them well.

Toward the end of the week, I was given a chance to go "into the field" to work with a cadaver dog and its handler. After our brief introductions, the handler, the dog "Spirit" and I set out with two other vehicles to the greater outskirts of Gulfport, going to streets near the coastline that had not been searched for victims. As buildings were searched there was a code that was painted on the outside wall, telling others if had been searched, the date, if it had been cleared, and so on. This saved repetitive efforts for those searching and recovering. One of the vehicles with us held members of ICE, federal officers who were armed and there for our protection. We didn't go out without an ICE vehicle or other police unit by our side. It was just too dangerous. Many areas were cordoned off with yellow tape; no one was allowed in unless it was official business. If you could prove you were a homeowner, you were allowed in for only twenty minutes to gather personal items, and then you had to leave. It was a dangerous time, for not only residents who had been displaced but for relief workers as well. Broken glass, shards of jagged metal, nails, electrical wire, all made you watch each and every step you took.

After about twenty minutes of work in the field by the cadaver dog Spirit, her handler would put the dog in an air conditioned van which followed us close by and actually I.V. the dog to bring her fluid levels to sufficient status. I had never seen or heard of such a thing. Spirit reacted with no nervousness or pacing. For her, it was just another day at work. I could imagine Spirit wondering, "Do I get some treats with that I.V?"

Spirit and her handler worked well together going from building to building, the dog going around the perimeter of each
78

structure. If the building was partially collapsed, Spirit would stick her nose into the structure to "test the air". We had searched several short streets, and after about four hours of non-productive work, the handler lovingly hugged Spirit and said "Let's call it a day girl. Time to rest." Spirit pulled gingerly on the twenty foot leash; she didn't have to be asked twice to quit.

The author deployed in Gulfport, Mississippi. He is seated by the "sign board" showing the way back north once the work in Gulfport was completed.

The super storm Katrina took a lot of lives, but not all the deaths we handled were by Katrina's hands. During the post death exam of one of the storm victims, an x-ray discovered a lodged bullet in the man's body. This certainly was not storm damage. Think about it, what a perfect time to commit a homicide. A person with murder in their mind might not think that every body found would be looked at closely, and thus, maybe a bullet wound would not be discovered? That was the error of his or her thinking. Upon finding of the bullet, the body was immediately taken to the state capital for further autopsy and investigation by the State Police. That victim first would have to be identified, notifications made to the family, then the proper police investigation into his death could resume. Another victim brought in had a money belt with $13,000 in it, which was immediately turned over to the authorities. Another man had a twenty-five caliber pistol tucked into his belt. Were both preparing for the storm but unable to escape its severity?

In New Orleans, it was a quiet peaceful Sunday morning, September 11th, four years after the attack on the Twin Towers and the Pentagon. Our commander called us all outside, where a minister held a prayer service to commemorate those killed years earlier at the Twin Towers. My mind raced back there, remembering again how I had spent says searching through debris on Staten Island. It seemed like it was just yesterday, not forty-eight months ago. Now, there was another tragedy for our country. Our morning prayer service was very somber, the morning sun streaming in and reflecting off the vestments being worn by the minister. We all bowed our heads quietly as he asked for our safety as we went about another day in our work to bring closure back to the families of those lost here. It was back to work.

Our work continued for a few more days, and our entire crew was anxious to be "debriefed" and allowed to go home. "Psych" personnel had to interview each of us one-on-one to make sure we were mentally ok after what we had seen and experienced. There is a high level of PTSD for people who are involved with combat, death, destruction, casualties, etc. It was the job of the psych personnel to see that we were going to be able to transition back into our normal everyday lives after leaving such death and destruction. That interview was one in which you didn't want to act a "little goofy" as we were told, and as I understand, all of our people took it seriously. We only acted goofy as we exited the room. We wanted to go home.

The flight back to Rochester a couple of days later brought me full circle back to my quiet, "normal", somewhat boring, day to day routine. Over the next few weeks, I would many times think about the man with the gold star inlay in his tooth, the man with the bullet in his chest, the unearthed corpse who had hopefully been identified and reburied, hoping for the day of the resurrection, not a tidal wave of water disturbing his slumber. May those who lost their lives and those who lost their loved ones eventually find peace. May those who are still lost be found and never unearthed again.

CHAPTER EIGHTEEN
FIT FOR A TRAVELING GUY

The distinguished gentleman who passed away had been a doctor in real life, and according to his well -mannered wife, had, for several years, practiced abroad in many different countries. He had been away from his native city for several decades, but his wife felt compelled to have him returned to his hometown for a graveside burial.

"He was a remarkable and learned man!" she exclaimed to me over the phone.

She continued singing her late husband's praises: "He will be missed by so many people, and he helped so many people with his skills."

She and her husband were both out of state at his passing, and after making several telephone inquiries to a funeral director near his death city, I had managed a plan to have him flown to me. The wife and I agreed to meet in a few days. We would then proceed with the local burial for those whom she wished to invite.

Several days passed, and the wife arrived at the funeral home exactly on the hour of our appointment, and we sat down to discuss his final disposition.

"He was a man of great means" she said.

I could see that by observing her. A striking woman in her seventies and well-dressed, from her blue two piece suit, matching shoes and jewelry, she did have a very well-taken-care-of appearance.

She produced a two page obituary from her white leather purse and plopped it in front of me, explaining, "I'd like this printed as it is written if you could. I know it will be quite expensive and all, but this truly was Richard, and I feel he deserves a good write up on his way out."

I scanned through the obituary. It was very lengthy indeed and spoke of his youth, his heritage, degrees earned, work background, and so forth.

"This might cost you in excess of two to three hundred dollars if we print it as is," I told her.

"Oh money is no concern you know. He made very good money in his life, and I'm going to be very well off in my last few years."

As she continued to explain to me what she wanted to be included at the graveside service, I was thinking about what I could offer her in a casket and vault that would befit such a professional man of his stature. I went through the itemization to show what she had committed in dollars to receive him back home for the burial. She had already committed several thousand dollars, but there was no expression of concern or shock on her face, so we proceeded to discuss the casket and vault for the cemetery.

As I started to make some suggestions to her on the merchandise, she interrupted me and said, "Stanley, just what is Richard in now, and would it be appropriate to bury him in that?"

I explained to her that Richard was in what we call a shipping container, made for the airlines. It is a double encasement of heavy duty cardboard reinforced with some light plywood and pine on the bottom and sides.

"Well, if he is already in that container" she remarked, "I can't see the need to remove him to a casket. I'm not going to dress him. No one is to see him. Can't we just leave him where he is and go from there?"

"Well," I responded, "I've never buried anyone in a shipping container before. It is going to have a few scratches and dents from the moving about, and it has a few postings and stickers on it from the airlines and the cities to which the transfers were made and so on."

Her smile was so wide, it was incredible. She was beaming as if she was a poor woman who had just hit the lottery.

"Oh!" she said, "Richard would love it, simply love it! It's like it was made for him. He traveled so much, and this container has travel stickers on it. I couldn't ask for more!"

I sat kind of perplexed, not because I wanted to make a big sale to her, as I was never much of a salesman in the selection room, but I thought Richard probably would have liked something a little more befitting to him in the end. However, the decision wasn't mine to make. We finished up with the wife selecting a simple concrete grave liner to be placed in the grave to hold Richard's shipping case.

The day of the graveside arrived, and my assistant and I placed the deceased on the lowering device over the grave, just as the minister drove in to make his short presentation. As the pastor went through the short service, my eyes scanned Richard's case and the stickers and writing which adorned it: "Head end", "handle with care, human remains", "Chicago O'Hare", "do not stack" , "Permit here", "fin.dest.Rochester." Final destination, alright. Richard's case certainly made for an interesting graveside service.

As the wife motored away through the cemetery gate, I couldn't help but ponder the week's scenario. One can never assume what someone is going to ask, request, or expect of you. And, in the end, when your travel ticket is finally punched, someone else will probably be making your final decisions for you...

CHAPTER NINETEEN

MILK MONEY

This day wasn't unlike any other day during my residency. The day had started with the usual delivery of flowers from a previous day's service. The cars were checked for fuel, the operating room given a quick overview for cleanliness and supplies in place. That is one thing that is always foremost in the mind of a good undertaker: you always had to be ready for the next call as you did not know when the phone would ring or what circumstances the phone call would reflect. And so, you were always ready, kind of like the firemen at the fire station, ready for the alarm to go off, and then you were off to the call, wherever it would take you, in a moment's notice.

And so it was on a typical day that the call came in from a local coroner who requested our presence at a home near Lake Ontario where a woman had died, unattended at her home. An unattended death in New York State always summoned a coroner or medical examiner. They would determine if and when an autopsy would be necessary, or, after talking to the person's doctor, if the body would be released directly to the undertaker who was called.

So it was on such a lovely sunny day that we put our removal stretcher into our grey station wagon to head to the scene, about thirty minutes north of the funeral home. Our wagon was always pristine, shined to the max, immaculate inside and out, window glass sparkling and bug free. In the days when station wagons were used for removals, the rear windows had to be black or darkened to some degree so the public could not see in. You couldn't have people gazing in to see a stretcher, let alone a stretcher with a deceased contained therein! The funeral business has always been, and still is, concerned with the sensitivities of those who watch what you do and how you perform both when you are out on a call and in the funeral home itself.

So the owner and I, dressed in short sleeved white shirts and narrow neckties, headed north to the scene, really not knowing what we would discover upon arriving. My boss, a skinny little guy at sixty, showed signs of the thirty plus years he had already invested in the business. As he lit up his usual cigarette, I lowered my window for some air. He smoked too much, especially when he got a death call. It calmed him, he said.

In a short time, we had arrived at the house. It was a dilapidated old farm house, the mailbox half off its rustic fence post it was attached to, the name on the box not even identifiable. As we drove to the front door, we saw the sheriff's car and another vehicle, the coroner I presumed. Both men stood on the front porch, it too showing signs of extreme age and wear. In its time, I am sure the house was magnificent, a huge old three story farm house, and in its shadow, two or three smaller out buildings. Yes, in its time, this must have been a wondrous place with its long tall windows and weathered oak door with its iron knocker, now frozen in place from lack of use.

My boss and I both recognized the coroner and the sheriff's deputy, and we exchanged pleasantries as we entered the home with our stretcher in hand.

"She's been living alone for years," said the coroner, "Husband's been dead over forty years according to the daughter. She's been kind of a hermit since he died."

The inside of the house was like a museum, furniture all appearing to be those pieces you see in an antique shop, including mantle clocks, not running but stilled by time and covered in dust. Most of the windows were draped, allowing little daylight into what must have been a very private life, a life now quietly ended in this cavernous house that felt so lonely.

We made our removal and took the deceased to the funeral home where she was embalmed, dressed, and made ready for burial. The daughter had made very simple arrangements, as she felt her mom had little money for anything elaborate. And so on a quiet day we returned the woman to a small cemetery not far from her home and buried her in with only three people in attendance.

About a week after the service and burial, we received a call from the coroner who had handled the case. My boss was sitting at his desk in the back room near where we did our work. He had a metal study light on an adjustable gooseneck that he could move around to illuminate his work. Again, the smoke hovered near the lamp head as he took the coroners call. After what seemed like only a minute or two of conversation, he put the black phone back in its cradle, shook his head and started laughing.

"What?" I said, wanting to know what I had just missed out on.

"Do you remember Marian from last week? The lady we pretty much buried as a pauper? Well, upon investigating the out buildings around the house, the coroner and the sheriff discovered an old milk can. Upon opening the can, they found over one hundred thousand dollars in cash in bills of all denominations, covered in mold and dirt. I guess she wasn't a ward of the county after all."

We couldn't believe it. Evidently the lady had just continued to put more and more cash into the milk can, choosing to live a life of just barely getting by. Her funeral had been a very meager one, but the final chapter was yet to be written. Upon hearing of the discovery of her mother's money, her daughter was moved to the extent that she purchased a very large and expensive grave marker to place upon the grave.

I revisited that grave site a few years later, and yes, there it was: a marker that was a true testimony to a fine lady. You can never judge what a person has on first discovery. Sometimes, you have to wait and see just how much milk money is saved for a rainy day.

CHAPTER TWENTY

THE TOOTH AND NOTHING BUT THE TOOTH

After many in the funeral business, I have come to believe that people lay awake at night thinking of a question that they perceive an undertaker has never been asked before. In one particular case, they succeeded.

I had pretty much finished making funeral arrangements with the immediate family of Harry, a man who had died the day before. We had written the obituary, gone over the financial statement, explained the cremation process, as this is what the family desired for the deceased. As we sat around the conference table exchanging pleasantries, one son turned to me and said, "Oh, by the way, we want to know if you can pull Harry's gold tooth out before you cremate him. He said he spent $1,300 on that tooth, and he didn't want it burned up."

The bells went off in my skull. Here indeed was another first, and this first was a dandy! Three decades and never a request for a tooth removal, but had I heard him correctly?

"You want me to remove his gold tooth?" I repeated, knowing that reflecting the question back to the sender was a sure step of getting the right information.

"Yep," said the son, "If you can just get 'er out for us we'll take it from there."

I explained to him that this was a request I had not had before and that I would try to give him an answer in the next twenty-four hours.

Soon after the family left, I checked the legalities. Undertakers are not licensed to do dentistry, only embalming and post death derma surgery for injuries. This was out of my realm. I called a local dental group, actually two. The receptionists both said, "You want our dentist to do what?" Both declined. One dentist did explain to me that the gold was dental gold, and that $1,300 was not for the metal itself, but rather for the whole package: fitting, casting, inserting, etc...

So, the next day, I explained my findings to the family, and they agreed to let Harry go with the tooth intact. It was an interesting twenty-four hours, to say the least. I still had my sanity. Harry still had his tooth.

CHAPTER TWENTY-ONE
APPARITIONS IN THE FRONT ROOM?

A fellow undertaker who was in business just eight miles from my firm would, from time to time, take his lovely wife and escape via airliner to the sunny part of the Carolinas. They would visit with some family there and just relax. I think they call that a vacation, a word not understood by many funeral home owners. You see, when you are in business in a small town and someone passes away, they want you, the owner, not another guy in a suit from a few miles away, to be there. It's a business like no other really. In many businesses, the owner isn't missed quite so much, but when you are entrusted to burying someone's dead, that tends to be very personal, as well it should be.

It was on such an occasion when I was covering for my friend, Ted, another local coroner, that his firm suddenly got quite busy. It could have been a death or two, possibly three, but it was summer time, and any number of deaths was sure to put a dent in your day's plan of mowing the lawn and painting the porch. There was always paint to put on when you owned your own funeral home. It was as though the weathering grinches came out almost nightly and made your newly painted project look old. They worked overtime putting dents and scratches into your new finishes, just so you could do the work over and over again. Entranceways always had to look pristine. The looks you would get from older ladies with their glasses on the tips of their noses if your porch was not "up to snuff" as the saying goes, could kill, pun intended. So if you owned a funeral parlor, it really owned you. You'd make a dime and put two back in. That was just the way it was.

Back to my narrative. Ted had gone away; now Stanley was on duty. After meeting with the family, making the arrangements and setting the schedule, things looked like they were pretty much in place for the next few days. It was a normal death, nothing noteworthy, except for day two, the day of the calling hours, which was tomorrow. What an odd day it would turn out to be.

The day of the calling hours arrived. The flowers were in place, and all was made ready for the family who would soon be in place. It was a magnificent summer's day. The sweet smell of grass and newly bloomed plants out front made you feel alive and ready to take on the challenges of the day. Soon, the family was in place in the reposing room, making ready to greet friends and relatives who would be arriving to pay their respects. Just before the first guests arrived, the daughter of the deceased woman came to me at the front door. She was as white as a ghost. She appeared quite shaken and her lower lip quivered as she spoke in a quiet tone.

"Stanley, there is something dreadfully wrong. The flowers on either end of the casket are shaking, moving if you will, and the curtain draped behind mom's casket is moving as well. I'm feeling quite faint actually."

I had her sit immediately, and I quickly strode into the reposing room, less than twenty feet away. I stopped ten feet from the casket and froze. My eyes moved left to right, up and down. There was nothing moving, nor did anything look out of place. I again rescanned the room. No, everything looked in order. Had this poor lady been so overwhelmed with losing her mother that she was feeling very anxious? Did she have a medical condition I wasn't aware of? I exited back to where she sat, and we talked briefly, all the time I was assuring her that all was well and it might have been just a draft moving through the funeral parlor.

About one hour later, a visitor came in and said, "Hey, did you feel the earthquake?"

94

I could not believe my ears. We had had an earth tremor? I hadn't noticed anything, and the glass chandelier over my head at the entrance way had not budged. Later, it was confirmed that a tremor had moved through several counties including ours, and it had only lasted a few seconds. The flowers and curtain moving at the casket were the result of that brief tremor. Upon leaving that day, the lady who had been so startled laughed it off: "I didn't really think the place was haunted," she joked, "but for a half a second, I did give it a thought."

CHAPTER TWENTY-TWO
GUNS, ROPES AND KNIVES

How many hundreds or thousands of ways are there to escape from this physical state we call life? I don't think anyone has ever tried to come up with a number, but the inventive spirit of people has amazed me over the years, not only in its simplicity, but also in its effectiveness in getting the job done. You would think most people contemplating either taking their own life or a life of another would seek to do it in a quiet fashion, in privacy, and not to be a burden to others. Oh how wrong those assumptions have been!

By far, the most popular instruments for immediate disposition to the next life are the gun and the rope. Most adults prefer a shotgun, the bigger the caliber, the more damage. The twelve gauge shotgun tucked under the chin and pointing at a 45 degree towards the rear is very effective in immediate death. The blast usually removes huge portions of the cranium, brain and surrounding tissues and makes for a horrific cleanup for those who are called in to attend to the death.

It was on a very nice fall day many years ago that a local coroner called me to assist with a death call of a man on a rural farm just eight miles to the east of my funeral home. Upon arrival there, we found the man, quite elderly and in bad health, having devised a plan to take his life, yet not to leave a mess for someone else to clean up. He had opened the kitchen window on the ground level and placed a shotgun on the sink, securing it so only the muzzle pointed out of doors. The man had then walked out of the house, fashioned a long stick to put into the trigger guard and, while placing his head to the muzzle, pushed the trigger of the gun, rapidly taking him to his maker. The blast was totally contained out of doors, with not a thing to be attended to in the house.

His family said later that he had always been thoughtful of others, and his final act kept true to form with the way he had led most of his life. The force of the gunshot had pushed the elderly man back a couple of yards from the house, and he laid face up in a green lawn, the purple blood stains encircling his remains, tissue and bone fragments scattered about within several more feet of where he quietly laid. We placed the man in a body bag, secured the projected pieces the best we could and made our way to the coroner's office, where a cause of death would have to be determined. I always got a kick out of that. A man's head could be missing, or he could be eviscerated on a buzz saw, and yet a pathologist would have to do an autopsy and determine a cause of death, and sometimes the obvious is not always the cause of death.

The most shocking kind of death, even to those of us who deal with death on a daily basis, is the sudden suicidal death of young people. Suicide rates among teens and young adults are fantastically high, the reasons not completely known or understood. Peer pressure, parent conflicts, drugs, alcohol, even teens making suicide pacts among themselves just for "something to do" takes huge numbers of people yearly. Could circumstances really be that bad for a person just to "do it" for the escape of a current situation they are in? Evidently, yes.

Many years ago, within a year after purchasing our rural funeral home, a young lady came to my door. She was dressed smartly in blouse, skirt, shoes and handbag and had a lost look on her face. She lived thirteen miles to our west, and when I asked her of her business at such a tender age, she replied, "My husband hung himself last night in my daughter's closet." I had hoped she was jesting, but a quick look around the otherwise empty porch told me no one had put her up to this; this was the real deal. I took her arm and escorted her inside to our smaller chapel where I seated her and prepared to hear her story.

As quickly as we had taken a seat, the young lady started her narrative: "Tom had been kind of distant lately, but I never in my mind thought that he would hurt himself." Her face was thin and drawn, her color ashen grey, and I knew her relating these facts to me was ripping her up inside. They only had been married a few years, had started a family, and were just beginning to live the dream that so many pursue at that young age.

"So we had dinner, some usual small talk, and had gone into the living room just to relax and watch TV. Our daughter, Jessie, was there with us. After an hour or so, Tom said he had to make a couple of phone calls. We have a bedside phone, and he headed in that direction, so I thought little of it. I became engrossed in the TV movie we had started. After about thirty minutes or so, I suddenly realized that Tom had not returned." Her body stiffened as she came to this part of the story.

"You don't have to continue if it's too difficult," I said to her.

"No…no" she insisted. I can't blot this out of my mind. It will be engraved forever in my head." She continued, "I walked down the hallway. Tom was not on the phone in our room, and I went further to Jessie's room and opened the door, peeked in, and saw nothing. I turned to leave, when I noticed her closet door partially open with the overhead light on. I walked to the door, and, as I took hold of the knob, my eyes saw Tom's arm."

Her head slumped, her face became flushed and a sigh was released as she began to whimper. "I called his name as I opened the door, but when I saw his face I knew he was dead."

I reached for a glass of water which I had nearby, and her trembling hands received it, almost spilling the contents as she raised it to her trembling lips.

"Let's stop for a few minutes," I said. "Then you can tell me what you'd like me to do for Tom."

After a bit of a break, we sat down and made his funeral arrangements. She opted for a turtleneck sweater to cover the deep mark left by the rope which Tom had used to end his life. Tom was a good looking young man with dark hair and a full beard. To view him in the casket, you never would have known that he himself had taken his own life.

The funeral was over, the family laid Tom to rest, and the wife now had the enormous task of trying to pick up the pieces and starting over again. Life can be so cruel, and death, it seems, is always waiting quietly in the wings, ready to take over at a moment's notice, and sometimes no notice is given. It just happens, again and again.

It was another autumn when our local coroner called, summoning me to a small settlement just three miles to the west of our village.

"Bring a heavy duty pouch, some extra gloves and a sheet if you have one handy" were his words. I knew immediately that when the coroner was requesting such equipment that the case I was going to help him with was probably not going to be a natural death. I piled the equipment on top of my stretcher, loaded it all into the station wagon and headed west, quite sure of the location that he had mentioned.

As I made a right hand turn up a county road, I could see the sheriff's car ahead, pulled to the side of the road, a couple of fellas standing in front of it smoking and jabbering as I pulled up and stopped.

"You can access the field right there" one man exclaimed as he pointed to a sluice pipe running through the ditch and just twenty yards ahead of me. I swung a wide right turn and guided the station wagon across the ditch and up a slight angle into the field, the engine kicking up some dust and ragweed as I motored ever so slowly up the incline.

As the station wagon pushed through the autumn hay and tall ragweed, I soon saw the coroner in his short sleeve white shirt and suspenders motioning me with his hand to keep coming to his location. My car hit a rock, which felt like it could be part of Alcatraz, and I mumbled a superlative in response to my sudden jolt upward into the ceiling. "Yeah," I thought, "Let's have Stan bring his car up through the field. Heaven knows we wouldn't want to jeopardize the coroner's precious vehicle."

Enough already. There was no time to be trivial, there was a deceased person here somewhere and we were being summoned to take part in his recovery. I jumped out of the station wagon, just in time to have the dust cloud which I had created completely devour me. Thank goodness I had stopped when I did. The deceased lay face down just another five yards in front of my car's front grill, and, yes, he appeared quite dead.

"Did you bring the heavy bag and some gloves?" inquired the coroner. "This guy is pretty heavy. He'll have to go to Rochester if you want the trip."

As I unloaded the equipment and neared the remains of the man, I couldn't help but notice what looked like a circle of red paint about ten yards in diameter, ending where the man laid. What was this about I pondered.

"Slashed his wrists with a jackknife, a dull jackknife, then he proceeded to walk in a circle till he dropped."

OK. Guess that pretty much explained it. Simple, effective, the cut and bleed will get the job done each and every time. The man was relatively young, in his forties, and came from a fine rural family. What a shame, and again there was the unanswerable question of why do people do such things?

A few days later, the man was buried in the Catholic cemetery just outside of town. The family dispersed, and just a few short years later his father passed away. His own death may have been hastened by the death of that son, but I guess we'll never know. Death is the great equalizer. It shows no boundaries, has no favorites, does not discriminate, and always, always has the final say.

CHAPTER TWENTY-THREE

AN ATTEMPT AT WAKING THE DEAD

Our funeral home was located at the corner of Church St. and Pleasant Avenue, both very quiet streets in this very small village tucked away in the foothills of the Southern Tier. On an average day, you could stand on the front porch and watch the small town folks going about their daily routines: a youngster riding the bike down the sidewalk, hurrying to the school playground just a block and a half to the north, an elderly lady walking down the same sidewalk on her way to pick up her mail on Main Street, one block to the west and an easy two minutes away. This truly was small town America.

The funeral I was planning for mid- morning was to be quite small, probably no more than thirty people or so. The woman who had passed was very elderly, with few family survivors left. She had outlived most of her friends and co-workers. She was a former school teacher. We were not going to proceed to the cemetery after the service. She was to be buried twenty miles away in a family plot with her husband who had passed away over thirty years ago. So being very at ease this day, I went to my daily duties of sweeping off the sidewalk and picking up the occasional piece of trash, which was quite rare to find on our street. It was going to be a repeat of another peaceful day, or so I thought.

Twenty minutes before service time, the small family arrived. I seated them in the chapel near the casket and had some very light piano music playing in the background. The deceased had enjoyed the piano herself, the family said, often sitting down at her old upright and playing for an hour or two nightly before retiring. We soon had what I had estimated: just under thirty mourners in the chapel as we awaited the arrival of the Methodist minister, who was just a half block from the funeral home. He would often arrive just moments before service time, scooting in at the last minute, knowing that I would have the speakers stand and microphone in place, anticipating his arrival. True to form, he arrived just three minutes before service time and handing me his slightly worn overcoat as he came through the front door.

"We all set?" he asked.

I nodded in the affirmative and replied, "I'll turn the music down. Your mic is on, and you can get started when you're ready."

The minister meandered up the aisle, bent over and remarked quickly to the next of kin before setting his notes on the podium. I was always stationed at the front door so I could receive anyone arriving late. From my vantage point, I could also look over the backs of those in attendance and see the minister as he performed his duties. Out of the corner of my eye, I spotted a village truck stopping at the corner of our intersecting streets. I didn't think it odd, as they were out and about all day around the village doing their daily maintaining of streets and sidewalks. I gave their arrival little more thought as the minister started his brief eulogy. As I set this scene, I must tell you that our chapel is very close, I mean within one foot of the sidewalk on Pleasant Avenue, so the casket is within five to six feet of the actual roadway. The minister had gotten to a very quiet part of his presentation and had asked those in attendance to bow their heads in prayer.

He went on to say, "In this quiet moment of this most peaceful day, we take this pause to remember the life of Helen."

Before he could utter the next sentence, the room started shaking from the reverberation of a jackhammer which was now pounding the pavement less than ten feet from where the speaker's podium stood. There were four pieces of flowers spread around the casket; their flowers and supporting greenery were vibrating wildly.

104

The drapery behind the casket was also responding, and not favorably, from the concussion that was emanating from the street. The minister's microphone was picking up the jackhammer's report and broadcasting it into the two rooms where speakers were connected. He stopped suddenly, looked up, and looked at me with this "what do I do now" look on his face. I raised one hand for him to stop. He smiled and nodded to the family as I raced out the front door, down the four steps and across the front lawn, all in one brisk leap that would have made the Olympics if I had been timed. The jackhammer operator saw me coming and eased off the machine, lifted his eye protection and uttered, "What?"

After a brief explanation that we had a service in progress, I told him to take his co-worker downtown for a coffee break, my treat, and give us twenty minutes to complete our work. He apologized, said he would be back in a minute and they retreated in the village truck as I had asked.

The service continued without further interruption, well almost. As we pulled out of the driveway a couple of hours later, we had to take a right onto the street as opposed to the usual left, as they had removed part of the pavement to work on a water line. I'm sure Helen didn't mind; it was an even more memorable day.

On the way out of the chapel, one of the mourners whispered to me, "Stan, next time maybe I better bring ear protection." He laughed gingerly as he exited the funeral home, which is certainly better than crying.

CHAPTER TWENTY-FOUR
SATURDAY MORNING DELIVERY

The year of my residency in upstate New York was an interesting one and quite exhausting as well. Those were the days that boasted no cell phones, lap tops, computers, etc.. A live person actually babysat the telephone 24/7 awaiting a death call. In the late 1970s, the first pagers actually came into use, giving the local undertaker some freedom to roam, but that in itself was limited communication.

Once your beeper went off, you had no idea what was on the calling end. Had someone died? Had the wife wanted you to pick up milk and bread on the way back from wherever you were? Then the real chore began: finding a pay phone, having the necessary change on you to call, hoping that whatever the call was, it was not urgent in nature, such as a coroner desperately awaiting your arrival to pick up someone who had just expired. Those were interesting days indeed, and before that, more challenging yet. In days of horses and buggies, the undertaker would just wait until someone came knocking on his door requesting his services, then he would head to the location to do his duty. So it was in this last part of the 20th century that great strides were made in rounding up the local digger.

It was a Saturday morning, quite early, just after 8 a.m., as I sat in the apartment over the funeral home having my toast when I heard the front door bell chime. My mind wasn't quite fully functional as I put the toast down. I didn't think we had anyone coming in at this hour, especially on a weekend, and the last family we had served had had their service a couple of days ago. Without further delay, I bolted down the majestic steps of the funeral home.

The steps, some twenty plus in number, had an ornate railing attached, which terminated just five feet from the front door. As I neared the main floor landing, I could see the shadow of a man standing on the other side of the frosted glass, his head bobbing from side to side. I assumed he was trying to look and listen for anyone who may have been summoned by his early morning entrance. As I tugged the massive door inward, the man jumped slightly, presumably startled by my quick response.

"Good Morning" I uttered. "Can I help you with something?"

The man, slightly bent from age and dressed quite simply in shirt, work pants, and a summer jacket, locked his eyes to mine. He started to speak, but seemed lost for a single word.

"Is David here?" he finally inquired.

David was my boss and owner of the funeral home and lived in the home adjacent to and at a 90 degree angle to the funeral home parking lot.

"Well, he's not in just yet, but I can call over for him if you like. Is it urgent?" I asked.

I could sense the man didn't want to talk to me, a stranger, about his needs.

"Well, my wife...she is...she has...well...I need to see David...could you get him for me?"

I looked at him straight away and said, "Could I have your name sir? I'll call him immediately."

"Tell him John Bailey from Ford Road is here. He knows me well."

I did a quick 180 turn and took two steps to a wall phone that was near the front door. After five rings, Dave picked up the phone and said he would be right over. I gently took the man inside and settled him into an oversized stuffed chair. He sat quietly, looking over the surroundings but made no further comments to me.

108

"Dave will be right along then" I said, and I closed the front door, knowing that Dave would come popping through the hallway after making his entrance from the rear of the funeral home. I didn't have long to wait. Within two minutes, Dave came briskly through the hallway, attired in short sleeve white shirt, pressed black pants and shined black dress shoes, laces tied even and tight. Before he reached the gentleman, Dave gave a big holler as his skinny right arm raised to wave hello.

"Well hello John!" he exclaimed. "What brings you to downtown this bright sunny morning?"

John stood, but his face did not reflect Dave's smile.

"It's Emily" John said. "I'm afraid she's...I'm afraid she's gone...I didn't know what to do...I got so confused...so I...well..."

Dave ushered him back into the overstuffed chair, his demeanor going from welcoming an old friend to sullen and serious.

"Just relax a minute John. Tell me what happened."

"I knew she was having a bad morning David, but I didn't think she was...that bad...she has a bad heart you know...just like her Mom had years ago. So, when we got in the truck this morning, she looked a little white, but she wanted to come to the market, so we headed out. Then about ten minutes ago, she got really quiet and just kind of put her head down on the back of the seat. I pulled the truck over and felt of her wrist. It was then that I knew she was gone."

David glanced at me. I sat ten feet away, within the shadow of our grandfather clock, listening to the story, not quite able to grasp what the man was telling us.

"Is she with you now John?" David asked.

"Yep. I'm so, so sorry. I didn't know what to do. I knew you'd be able to help me."

John's head slumped. His hands shook as he held his head, the tears streaming onto the summer jacket that looked worse for the wear. The tears were infectious, and I felt the first one leave my eye and hit my lip, its salty flavor telling me here was death brought to our door on a Saturday morning.

Dave instructed John to stay seated, as he grabbed my arm and we headed for the front door. Down the four front steps we ran to the old brown and grey pickup parked out front. Dave opened the front seat, and their sat John's wife, Emily, looking much like she was napping, her violet flowered dress tucked neatly under a tan shawl which engulfed her like an old friend. Dave touched her neck, feeling for a pulse as he told me to call the police and an ambulance.

Within minutes, the parking lot was filled with emergency vehicles: lights flashing and ambulance attendants in white coats. But there was no hurry; Emily was gone. The police called the local coroner, who meandered by a short time later to pronounce her dead. He was also a local doctor who John and his wife and was aware of Emily's medical history. Emily was gently removed from the vehicle and placed on our stretcher and taken through the parking lot into our garage and up a ramp into our preparation room. This was a Saturday morning delivery like no other. You see, when you are living over a funeral home, the next doorbell ring could be...well, let's wait and see.

CHAPTER TWENTY-FIVE
BETTER THAN WINNING THE LOTTERY

You keep thinking as a funeral director that no one could surprise you with a question that you've never been asked before, but decade after decade in this industry, the general public has continued to formulate new questions, or at least re-writes on the same questions, adding maybe a new twist or two. And sometimes, people will actually shock you as to their vision of what they want for themselves or their loved ones when "that time" comes. This next little gem happened many, many years ago, and that vision, or planning for the future, actually panned out on the plus side of the equation.

The lady who appeared at my door at mid-morning on that August afternoon was a local gal I had seen around town. I knew her face but didn't have a name that I could attach to her. As I opened the oak front door of the funeral home, she politely introduced herself and explained that her mom had died earlier that morning at the hospital.

"It wasn't that long ago," she said, "and I thought I'd just stop by as opposed to calling you."

I ushered her into the front room where my desk was and apologized for wearing casual clothes, as I had been planning to accomplish some outside tasks on such a nice day. We talked for some time about her mom, and her brother and sister, one of each if my memory serves me right. She said her mom had purchased a couple of graves at a small cemetery just a mile and a half outside of town about ten years ago when her father died. I knew the place about which she talked. There was a small holding vault there, and, from time to time in the winter, we had to store a casket or two there to wait for better burial conditions in the spring.

After about an hour, we had completed the arrangements for her mom. It was to be a direct burial, maybe a graveside prayer, but no preparation of the body, just dressing and casketing and a burial when we could get the grave opened.

When we arrived at the time for her to pick out a burial vault which her mom's casket would be buried in, she paused for a moment and said to me, "We purchased moms' vault when dad died ten years ago. The cemetery guy said the graves were up under a very large tree, and he thought it would be easier because of the tree roots to try to bury both of the vaults at the same time, just because of the obstructions."

"Okay," I thought. So we have dad buried under the tree a decade ago, and his wife's vault buried empty next to him.

I excused myself quickly, as I wanted to find her father's file to see what type of vault was used for the both him and her mother. You see, most burial vaults, but not all, have a liner and/or seal around the top to impede water going into them over the years. Other concrete containers or grave liners have no such protective measures, and thus little or no protection other than shielding the casket from the weight of the earth above it.

I soon located her dad's file. Quickly thumbing through the paperwork, I discovered that the merchandise used indeed, was grave liners, not grave vaults. Returning to the daughter's side, we continued our discussion about the graveside service she wanted to schedule a few days into the next week.

"Is there a stone marking their graves?" I asked. She paused a few moments, as she reached into her purse to retrieve a day planner.

"There was a small slant monument put up a couple of years after dad passed, but the guy who erected the stone put it at the wrong end of the graves, at the foot rather than at the head, so the cemetery guy went ahead and re-positioned the monument, so I think it's in the right spot now."

WOW. I'm rubbing my forehead as I'm thinking, "Okay, we have a body in place in one grave, plus an empty grave liner buried next to him, but we are not sure which grave liner is in which grave?"

This could be very interesting when it comes time to make a burial next week. Soon after our discussion ended, the gal scurried out of the funeral home and down the front steps, as I reached for the phone to try to locate my grave digger.

The fellow who was to open the grave had his own construction company where he worked during the day, so it was twilight when I reached him. He agreed to meet me the next morning at graveside to look the situation over. It was to be a long night.

I couldn't help but think, "Are we going to dig up a man who has been buried for ten years, or will we luck out and unearth the empty grave liner and hopefully not have it be full of water? Neither choice sounded too attractive, but I certainly hoped the latter would be the case.

It was a grey sky with just some light mist in the air when I awoke the next morning. I quickly dressed and jumped in the car and made the short drive to the cemetery to meet my guy there so we could do some exploratory wok on the grave we were to open. He hopped out of his truck and met me under the big tree where the graves were located.

"There seems to be a little bit of confusion where each is buried here. I understand that one of these is the husband; the other grave contains an empty grave liner" I said.

"Well," he uttered, "I wasn't here when the husband was buried, but maybe we can take a steel bar, drive it down to the top of the liners and try to determine which one is occupied and which one is empty."

"What a great idea," I thought. This could actually work.

"The other alternative," he suggested, "is to just dig one up, pop the top, and see what's there or not."

This choice didn't sound that appealing to me, but if this one was the choice we were going to make, we had a 50-50 chance of getting it right.

He went to his truck, procured the steel bar, about five foot in length, and returned to the grave. I stood back as he started to pound the bar into the grave with his ten pound sledge hammer. After about two feet or so, he struck solid concrete.

"I'm on top of the liner now," he said. "Why don't you put your ear on the ground next to the bar, and I'll tap it some more, see if you hear any kind of an echo back, see if it sounds real solid or empty."

Now here was another first: my ear pressed against the ground, in the leaves and dark grass, listening for a return of his sledge hits as he tapped lightly on the bar.

"It sounds solid," I said, "but I'm not hearing anything but you hitting concrete."

"Let's go to the grave next to it and do the same," he suggested as he twisted and pulled the bar out of the ground.

We repositioned ourselves three feet to the right, directly over the accompanying grave, and we proceeded to duplicate what we had done previously.

"I'm not hearing any difference in sound," I reported to him. "They both sound about the same."

"Well, I guess the proof in the puddin' will be to uncover one, and pray for the best."

"Pray" indeed was the key word here.

My grave digger went to his tractor, which he had brought in the night before, fired the beast up, and gently rolled it over to the two graves where I stood. The mist was getting a little heavier now, and a light wind had started, making for quite a dreary day in the cemetery. The digger had told me he would not charge me extra for the exploratory, as he knew the family that had called me, and explained he would only have to go down two feet or so to get the top totally cleared. Then we would put a chain on the lid and gently raise it to make our discovery.

The front of the shovel gently peeled back the first few inches of grass and topsoil, as I stood witness a few feet away. As he filled the bucket, he would swing to the left, away from both graves and deposit the dirt nearby for easy retrieval. After about fifteen minutes, he had exposed the entire lid of the grave liner. He shut down the engine, jumped off the tractor, and jumped into the grave, landing squarely on top of the concrete lid.

"Doesn't look any worse for the wear after ten years," he remarked.

There was no seal between the lid and the body of the liner, so it was just academic in prying the lid a few inches upward to look inside the box.

"So," he said, "you want to do the honors or you want me to take a look?"

As he was uttering the last part of his sentence, the rain started to get a little heavier. Not quite enough to make you wet, it was more of a nuisance rain.

"I'm hoping this is the empty one," I said, "and if the stone has been properly placed, this should be the empty one, and, if it is, let's hope it's not full of water."

He placed the crowbar between the lid and the box, pushed down on it with a hefty grunt, and I saw the lid make a gradual nudge upward. I was on my hands and knees now, peering down into the grave, hoping I would see blank space, not a casket that had been interred ten years before. As the light dirt gave way around the edges, the lid moved upward another two or three inches. And there I saw...emptiness!

Success! He had uncovered the right one, and the best news was that it was dry as a bone in the middle of a desert. We both smiled broadly, knowing our mission was accomplished. All he had to do now was to cover the open grave with some plywood and lumber and wait for the burial, which would take place in a couple of days.

Some days things go just right. Those days make up for the days when your plans slide downhill and get worse from there. We loaded our equipment and headed for the local coffee shop. Today, it would be my treat. One chance in two worked out for a change, and it felt better than having a winning lottery ticket.

CHAPTER TWENTY-SIX
LET'S NOT BURY THE TRUCK...

What a terrific day for a funeral! The sun was high in the bright blue sky; the grass was green and just recently tended. Everything looked in place for the 2:00 pm funeral scheduled at the funeral home. Who knows how or when the magical hour of 2:00 pm was selected some decades back. Everyone wanted to be buried at 2:00 pm. Why? You sit around all morning, waiting for the hour to arrive, pretty much losing a day's opportunity to do other things. Traditions are odd; many just don't make any sense. And in the winter, a 2pm funeral barely gives you enough time to get to the cemetery and fill the grave before twilight is upon you. But on a day like today, you didn't worry about fading light. It was a robust day of summer. The kids were on their bikes being chased by their favorite hounds, and the lady Doris, the village sentry down the street who kept track of everything and everybody in town, was in her methodical shuffle to the post office to get her mail, the highlight of her lonely day.

At noon, the flowers arrived and were arranged in the front room, the parlor checked for cleanliness, tissues and general suitability, and the family quickly arrived to take their stations around the casket. The procession to the small cemetery, less than a mile from town, was casual, orderly, and respectful. These were the days when people actually pulled over out of respect for the deceased. They weren't in a hurry, like today when they speed by you to go and snatch their awaiting pizza. As we processed into the cemetery, the cars drove under the old and ornate horseshoe sign that welcomed them to ValleyBrook Cemetery. You couldn't help but wonder what year and day had that been set? Did the man who erected that sign a hundred years ago rest here? That might be an interesting tidbit to delve into on a quiet day, but at hand right now was the grave side service and a carload of flowers awaiting delivery to the cemetery and a few local nursing homes.

After the grave side prayer and a quick supervision of the family as they drove from the cemetery, I looked up to see the local grave digger, Pete, coming through the gate in his old pickup truck. Beside him was his faithful little dog who was usually tagging along, probably just to make sure Pete did the job right.

"Pete," I said, "I have a carload of flowers at the funeral home, so I'm going to go load them, and I'll be back shortly."

"Take your time," replied Pete, as he started to retrieve his tools from the rear of the truck. With a quick glance, I noticed he had a pretty good load of dirt on the truck he would be using to help back fill the grave.

As I wheeled out of the cemetery and headed back to the funeral home, I couldn't help but notice a few lingering relatives who had moved to the back of the cemetery, inspecting, I presumed, some old family headstones. When I ran up the back ramp and into the parlor, it was like always: chairs scattered and in disarray, lights still on full, a co-mingling of large and small flower arrangements scattered around the bier where the casket had reposed just thirty minutes earlier. How could a room that looked so good be so destroyed in such a short time? The cleanup could start later, I thought, as I fumbled for the flower list in my coat pocket.

"Let's see. What goes where?" There were at least eight pieces going to grave side, the others to nursing homes just eight miles away. In a few moments, I had tucked all the pieces into the back of the car, securely snugging them together in cardboard and bricks to keep them from tipping, falling over, and breaking.

Within minutes, I was back in eyesight of the grave, which was in the process of being filled, but I wasn't quite sure of what I was witnessing. As I pulled into the drive, I saw Pete, standing next to the grave, his hands on his hips, looking dismayed. The rear wheels of his truck were not visible. The front of his truck was inclined about 45 degrees with the front wheels 10 to 12 inches off the ground. As I jumped from the car and ran to the site, I couldn't help but smile. This I had not seen before. In his attempt to back the truck to the grave and dump the dirt load, Pete had gotten a little too close. The rear wheels were dropped into the grave and were now resting on top of the cement vault, which contained the dearly departed.

"Did you get a little close there Pete?" I inquired.

Pete removed his sweat-lined ball cap, rubbed his forehead with a hand twice the size of mine, and said, "Yeah, a little close I guess. It sure looked different in the mirror." We both broke out in a loud laugh that panicked the dog into running circles about us, the open grave, and the half-buried truck.

Pete's son soon popped in to check on his Dad, saying simply, "Old man, we need to get your glasses checked."

His son soon had Pete hooked up and pulled out, and we proceeded with the task of filling the grave. The eight flower pieces plus the casket and stand-up spray were arranged as a flower blanket on top of the grave, and our day was completed.

That weekend, I happened on Pete and his son enjoying coffee together at a local coffee shop. His son was announcing to everyone in the place, "Did you hear Dad is trying to get rid of his truck?"

His laugh bounced off the walls, as the waitress brought the doughnuts. "Next time, let's not bury the truck, okay Dad?"

CHAPTER TWENTY-SEVEN

A BEAGLE IN CHURCH (DAY OF THE BEAGLE)

My assistant and I arrived at the Methodist Church in plenty of time for the scheduled 1:00 pm memorial service. We unloaded the five floral pieces and placed them appropriately around the altar and the riser in front of where I would be seating the family.

The gentleman who had passed just three days earlier had been cremated, and his lovely wife, also getting on in years, had decided she would like his service at their church where they had been married some forty- five years earlier. This is truly the full circle of life, being baptized at a church, perhaps being married at the same altar a couple of decades later, and finally having your mortal remains taken to the same facility for a final goodbye. What would transpire at that altar less than an hour from now was another of those "it will never happen again" moments, a moment indeed worth writing about.

The church members started to arrive within twenty minutes of the appointed hour, and I briskly assisted them at the register book, handing them a service bulletin and directing them to a seat. One elderly lady with a rough looking fox wrapped about her neck whispered in my ear as she passed, "Do you fellows have Mrs. Billings who passed away last night? She was a dear and I must know where she will be laid out."

Having no knowledge of the woman's death, I remarked back to her, "I'm so sorry, but no, our firm has not been notified of her passing. Perhaps one of the other firms in town has her."

"Oh quite so" she uttered back. "Although, your firm does such a lovely job, can't see anyone wanting to go elsewhere."

Before I could suggest she look at the evening newspaper, she had quickly left my left ear and had made her way through the double doors at the back of the church. She was heading for one of the nearby ancient wood pews, which had no padding, just a straight back and a most uncomfortable contour. I had figured out years ago why so many churches built a century ago configured them as such. It would be very difficult, if not impossible, to fall asleep in one of these pews. Even if a man or woman of the cloth were to go on for an hour, or more, you most assuredly would have to be constantly manipulating your back and limbs to keep from seizing up. This surely would keep you awake through the majority of the sermon delivery!

Within twenty minutes, we had almost seventy people in church. The pastor winked at me on his way in and said, "Good day young man. I'll try to be brief today." Now when a Pastor says that, be prepared. What that means is that you will be there for the duration. In fact, you might miss your first child's birth.

Soon, the pastor was at his post, and the organist had sounded the official opening with his rendition of "The Old Rugged Cross". To my left, came two very young and distinguished looking members of the U.S. Navy. The deceased had been a Veteran of the Navy, and these folks were here to present the flag to his wife who now sat in the first pew on the right. I instructed them on where the wife was seated, what she was wearing etc.. They stretched their necks to make sure they had her in sight and nodded in the affirmative to me. I thanked them in advance for their service and they said in return to me, "You're welcome Sir. We are honored to be here today."

The pastor had finished his sermon and from the pulpit announced that military honors would now be accorded before the final blessings given. The two service people walked slowly in step up the middle aisle of the church. Their actions together, almost forming one person. Military honors were always moving, seeing the flag unfolded, refolded and handed to a loved one, thanking them for the veteran's service to the nation. But today, there would be a little icing on the cake.

As the service attendants held the flag fully unfolded and prepared for the re-fold, out of a secondary parallel aisle to the left came running the unmistaken brown, black and white dog body of a small Beagle. He hit the main aisle, made a sharp left turn and bolted for the front of the church. As he passed three rows of pews, several in attendance started to laugh, a sharp contrast to the seriousness of the two Navy personnel who looked on, trying to keep their composure. As the Beagle passed the eigth and ninth aisles, a gentleman on the very inside reached down, grabbed the Beagle and gingerly pulled him up on the pew, putting to an end to his uninvited presence at this most solemn occasion.

I believe the widow never knew what happened behind her, and the flag presentation was completed with all its dignity that could be mustered. We never did find out who the dog belonged to, but everyone in attendance had a smile on their face as they left. I'm sure many were thinking that this was not an accident, but rather planned by a "Higher Up" authority to lessen the pain of those in attendance. If it was HIS will, it worked. After all, who couldn't love a Beagle in church.

CHAPTER TWENTY-EIGHT

REFLECTIONS AND PREDICTIONS

Funeral service is changing rapidly, and, unfortunately, not for the better. Like other rituals of the twenty first century, it is reflective of how society looks at itself, and "self" is the new norm. For the past two hundred years, death was handled as a family event. A person died and was usually embalmed and mourned for several days. This was followed by a funeral and burial befitting their respective lifestyle. Embalming was the norm then. This is no longer the case.

Dr. Thomas Holmes, known as the father of embalming, invented most common embalming techniques. Holmes himself embalmed hundreds of Civil War men killed in action so their remains could be sent home for a proper burial. Soon after his early actions, mortuary schools opened around the country to teach his procedures and skills. Many still operate today, teaching new students of funeral service not only the art of embalming, but also all other aspects of taking care of families who are in need.

But today, fewer people are choosing embalming of their loved ones. Younger people today, usually those under age forty, are very much concerned about their "carbon footprints", the contamination we are leaving behind us, such as embalming chemicals, concrete or steel vaults, and caskets. People are now concerned with all these things being buried and eventually decaying and affecting the eco-system. Because of the new thoughts on funeralization in general, people are now leaning more toward cremation. As a result, cremation rates are growing steadily upward. On the west coast, 50% to 60% of all deaths are cremation. On the

East Coast, a strong 40% of deaths are cremation, and this number is growing annually.

But cremation is not for everyone. Having a loved one placed in a crematory for two to three hours at eighteen hundred degrees is for some people, almost sacrilege. Add to it the mix of dozens of different religions each with their own beliefs, and this makes for some interesting dilemmas for sure. There are sound economic reasons for those considering cremation. It is much less expensive than what we call the traditional funeral, but more than the economics, it reflects today's lifestyle.

Decades ago, people would take three, four, five days to commemorate a death. This kind of time is almost non-existent in today's age. People are rushed, stressed, busy with jobs, sports, hobbies, and the list goes on. Churches, service clubs, volunteer ambulance corps and fire departments are all feeling the pinch in membership numbers and people who want to step up. People get home, shut the door and want time for themselves. We are a self-indulgent society. Going out and fraternizing is not common, like it was years ago. When did you hear last of a neighbor going to visit a neighbor after the evening meal, just to catch up on things? The evening meal is another tradition absorbed by the high tech age. The funeral tradition is also being peeled away, like so many other important societal events. After a death, some want little or no visitation, some little service or no service at all, more and more often, a direct burial or cremation. Many people are even shunning the word "funeral" for the new term "life celebration" and with these "celebrations" come trappings of balloons, pictures, videos, mementos or collections of the deceased's things.

And why not? This is what it's all about: celebrating the life that is now over. The days of solemn organ music in dim lit chapels with the deceased laid out amongst flowers is soon to be history itself. And maybe that's a good thing. Evolution in the way we do things in all aspects of our lives comes about every few decades and from one generation to the next. Death indeed is the great equalizer.

126

Whether you are the destitute street person or the millionaire Wall Street broker, we are all equal once driven through that cemetery gate, a fact many never consider. In the future, how will we remember someone's life? Will we even take time to remember that life? A statement I heard years ago has always stayed with me: "a life not remembered is a life not lived." How true that is. So, let's humbly stop and reflect where we are going, and when we get to that place in time, can each of us answer the question, "Did I take the right road? Did I do the right thing?" Let's hope we all answer in the affirmative. Let's hope that our lives are worth remembering and celebrating...

UNDERTAKINGS OF AN UNDERTAKER

TRUE STORIES OF BEING LAID TO REST